ERIC MONKMAN
is from Oakville, Ontario, Canada. He has studied (and quizzed) at the University of Waterloo, the University of Toronto and the University of Cambridge. When he lived in Ottawa to work for the Canadian government, he quizzed there too. He is known for his intense concentration and his emphatic delivery.

BOBBY SEAGULL
was born in East Ham and is studying for a doctorate in Education specialising in Maths alongside teaching Maths at Chesterton Community College. He worked as a financial trader at Lehman Brothers, and qualified as a Chartered Accountant at PwC. He is also co-founder of OxFizz, an educational social enterprise, and a trustee of the charity UpRising, a youth development leadership organisation.

The pair are good friends, and became famous after appearing on series 46 of BBC Two's *University Challenge*.

First published in 2017
by Eyewear Publishing Ltd
Suite 333, 19-21 Crawford Street
London, W1H 1PJ
United Kingdom

Printed in England by TJ International Ltd, Padstow, Cornwall

Nobody's Perfect: if you spot any errors we've made,
please contact us at info@eyewearpublishing.com

ISBN 978-1-911335-99-3

WWW.EYEWEARPUBLISHING.COM

ERIC MONKMAN &
BOBBY SEAGULL

WITH CARTOONS BY MICHAEL CHESTER

EYEWEAR PUBLISHING

TABLE OF CONTENTS

PREFACE • 7

DEDICATION • 9

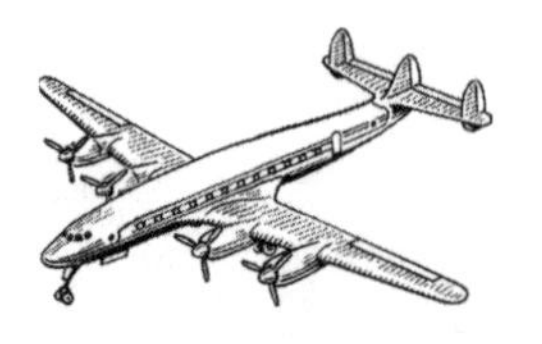

STARTERS • 11

30 Starter For 10s • 12

60 Bonus Questions (20 sets of 3) • 26

CATEGORIES OF QUESTIONS • 51

SPORTS • 52

10 Words In The Name
Of British Football Clubs • 54

20 Sports Time • 60

ARTS AND HUMANITIES • 71

10 Red, Yellow and Blue – The Arts • 72

10 Literature • 78

10 English Words of Non-Indo-European Origin • 84

10 Names Of Books In The Old Testament
Of The Bible • 89

11 Words That Are Associated With Colours • 94

MATHS AND SCIENCE • 101

10 Maths And Science • 102

10 Units • 108

10 Equations & Statements (mix/match) • 113

10 Discredited Theories • 117
10 No Diminishing Returns to Knowledge! –
Business, Economics and Finance • 123

HISTORY • 129
4 Parallel Lives • 130
10 The Road To D-Day • 133
10 National Days • 139
10 Before 1000 BC • 145

MISCELLANEOUS KNOWLEDGE • 151
20 The Price of a Pint of Milk - Pop Culture • 152
10 'Best Picture' Winners of the
Past 10 Years • 163
10 Non-Capital Cities • 168
20 Amazing Women • 173
15 Colleges of Oxford • 184
20 6.48 a.m. Puzzle for *Today* (and Tomorrow) • 191

DIFFERENT FORMS OF QUIZ • 199
19 Connection Questions • Starting at 199
48 Pub Quiz • 200
10 Newspaper Quiz • 215
50 Primary School-Level Questions • 218

CHRISTMAS

20 All I Want For Christmas Is...
Christmas-Themed Quiz Questions • 243

THE FINAL CHALLENGE

40 Buzzer-Style Trivia Tossups (10 questions, each followed by 3 bonuses) • 253

ANSWERS! • 275

CONCLUSION • 310
ACKNOWLEDGEMENTS • 312

PREFACE

This book is best enjoyed with friends (though we wouldn't blame you if you tried these questions by yourself). Part of the fun of quizzing is seeing how you do in comparison to others. The satisfaction of knowing something (*What's the capital of Burkina Faso?*, for example, or *who invented the micro-wave?*) when everyone else on your team draws a blank is part of what has made pub quizzing a national pastime in the UK. And who doesn't enjoy seeing whether you know more than the contest-ants on a quiz show? Certainly both of us were pleased after our matches when people told us how many answers they got when watching. It was like being able to enjoy your favourite hobby with people across the whole country!

The two of us first met as part of a quiz at Cambridge University. Bobby Seagull had arranged some practice matches, in which Eric Monkman competed. Our friendship pretty much grew out of a shared love of trying to see *who* knew *what*. We had the chance to go head-to-head, buzzer to buzzer, against each other for our teams (Emma-nuel College and Wolfson College) for just under 30 minutes on TV at 8pm Monday 27th March 2017. It was an exciting match, but Wolfson ulti-mately prevailed in *University Challenge*'s tightest semi-final for twelve years (Bobby has since forgiven Eric for this, especially as Eric had the chance to meet world-famous theoretical physicist Stephen Hawking in the grand final!).

We still enjoy quizzing each other. In fact, Bobby even has a special way of tearing and folding a newspaper around the daily quiz to make looking up the answer easy. We do not always get all the answers between us (Bobby needs to work on his Greek & Latin word roots and Eric on his sporting knowledge), nor do we always win pub quizzes (they often require a different knowledge set than the one we needed on television). But we always have fun quizzing together, and now we get to quiz you.

Good luck!

Bobby Seagull and
Eric Monkman

DEDICATION

Eric: This book is dedicated to my mother Deborah Badowski, my original fan.

Bobby: I spent a lot of my childhood Saturday afternoons in East Ham library, sprawled across the floor with books ranging from the history of the Aztecs, to Roald Dahl's fiction, to science and the solar system. My papa, Jose, used to take me, my elder brother Davey and my younger brother John as a regular pilgrimage. My youngest brother Tommy had to wait a few more years before his library adventures began. And my mum, Jamma, would have some south Indian food waiting for us at home after we were tired out by reading (and ready by 4.45pm, just in time to listen to the final football scores!) I'd like to dedicate this quiz book to my family and to all the books that opened my eyes to the world.

Eyewear: We'd like to thank Robert Gwyn Palmer, agent, for being so helpful during this book's creation, and Catherine Flanagan for her expert Quiz master eye.

STARTERS

CHAPTER 1: 30 STARTER FOR 10s

These are typical starter questions to begin the book. You can choose to do them all at once; or play University Challenge*-style, and for any correctly answered question, go forward to any of the sets of three bonus questions in Chapter 2; or any of the sets of 10+ 'category' questions later in the book. If you get a question wrong, you've lost your chance to answer any more questions until the next turn. Good luck!*

1

'Any sufficiently advanced technology is indistinguishable from magic.' This is one of the three laws formulated by which British writer? Born in Somerset in 1917, he became famous for co-writing the screenplay for the 1968 film *2001: A Space Odyssey* and as the author of the novels *Childhood's End, Rendezvous with Rama* and *The Foundations of Paradise*. Alongside Robert Heinlein and Isaac Asimov, he is known as part of the 'Big Three' of science fiction. He died in Colombo, Sri Lanka in 2008.

2

What single digit links: the number of Galilean moons; in mathematics, the fourth root of 256; in Buddhism, the number of Noble Truths; and in chemistry, the atomic number of the element beryllium?

3

'He speaks to me as if I were a public meeting.' According to biographer George Russell, these were the words of complaint by Queen Victoria about which of her Prime Ministers? Born in 1809 in Liverpool, he was a campaigner for Home Rule for Ireland. Identify this former Liberal Prime Minister, whose career lasted over 60 years and who was not only Britain's oldest PM, but served that role on a record four occasions.

4

German Bartholomeus Strobel and Italians Titian and Caravaggio are among artists who have painted which biblical event? This distasteful incident was ordered by Herod Antipas at a dinner party, acting on the request of his stepdaughter Salome. He may have been named Antipas, but the guests were not likely to savour the first course...

5

Name this animal: the only living relative of the giraffe, this animal is native to the canopy forests of the northeast of the Democratic Republic of the Congo. First described in 1901 by English zoologist Philip Sclater, it derives part of its full classification name from the British governor of Uganda, Sir Harry Johnston. It could be a missing link between giraffes and zebras: much smaller than its long-necked cousins, at 1.5m at shoulder, and with striped black-and white legs standing out below a reddish-brown body. The mule (half-horse, half-donkey) can eat its heart out.

6

Citing her work in 'the dynamics and geometry of Riemann surfaces and their module spaces', what is the name of the Iranian mathematician who was the first female winner of the Fields medal in 2014, and died of cancer in July 2017?

7

Excluding the Vatican City and Rome, what are considered to be the two closest capital cities between two sovereign countries? The first of these capitals is named after Italian-French founder Pierre Savorgnan de Brazza; the second is renowned for hosting the Ragnarok of boxing matches in 1974 – the 'Rumble in the Jungle' between George Foreman and Muhammad Ali. Name these two capitals, separated by just a few kilometres on either side of the Congo River.

8

E-coli, the bacteria, is short for 'Escherichia coli'. Give the dictionary spelling of the word *Escherichia*.

9

Yet to be discovered in 1871 and hence given the provisional name of 'eka-manganese' by Dmitri Mendeleev, what element was finally discovered in 1937? It became the first predominantly artificial element to be produced, with atomic number 43.

10

'It is better to light a candle than to curse the darkness'. This is the DIY motto of which non-governmental organisation, founded in 1961 in the UK by lawyer Peter Benenson? Following the publication of the article 'The Forgotten Prisoners' in *The Observer*, this organisation was founded to 'conduct research and generate action to prevent and end grave abuses of human rights'.

11

Benfica in 1962, Inter Milan in 1965, Ajax in 1973, Bayern Munich in 1975, Liverpool in 1978, Nottingham Forest in 1980, AC Milan in

1990 and most recently Real Madrid in 2017, have achieved what rare feat in the European club football's leading competition, the European Champion Clubs' Cup or Champions League?

12

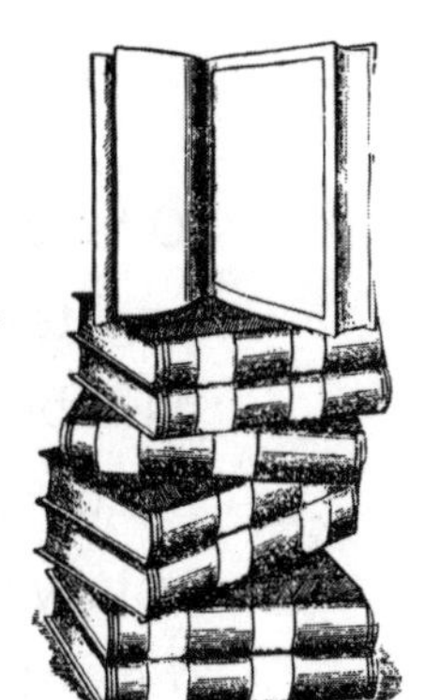

What six-letter word links: a bird found in most tropic and subtropical regions, known as *psittacines*; the second word of the title of a 1984 Booker Prize-nominated novel by Julian Barnes; and a style of repetitive rote learning often associated with Victorian-era schools?

13

What building is described by the organisation Historic England as 'universally recognised as one of the key buildings of the modern epoch'? Completed in 1986, it was designed, like the Pompidou Centre in Paris, with key features such as staircases, lifts and water pipes on the outside and hence is sometimes known as the 'Inside-Out Building'. Outside staircases could cause accidents for its inhabitants, particularly in an 88m-high building (the antenna spire taking its total height from 88m to 95m). Luckily they're covered over in its iconic metallic design. Name this building, created in London by Richard Rogers & Partners.

14

'O for a muse of fire, that would ascend the brightest heaven of invention.' Believed to have been written around 1599, these are the opening words to the prologue of which history play by Shakespeare, which focused on the events immediately before and after the Battle of Agincourt?

15

The Italian composer Rossini, describing this symphony, said, 'What a good thing this isn't music.' The events described in the symphony were summarised by American Leonard Bernstein: 'you take a trip, you wind

up screaming at your own funeral.' Subtitled 'An Episode In The Life Of An Artist', and with a less popular sequel *Lélio*, what was this symphony written in 1830 (as Bernstein points out: perhaps under the influence of opium) by French composer Hector Berlioz?

16

'There is no reason to believe that bureaucrats and politicians are better at solving problems than the people on the spot.' These are the words of which American political economist, born in 1933 in Los Angeles? In 2009, the Nobel Prize in Economics cited this economist's work during the award for an 'analysis of economic governance, especially the commons'. Passing away in 2012, identify this woman; the first woman to win the Nobel Prize in Economics.

17

Founded in 1842 in St Petersburg, this company or firm was nationalised by the Bolsheviks in 1918. This jewellery firm is now most renowned for designing elaborate jewel-encrusted eggs. (Everybody's good at something.)

18

'A custom loathsome to the eye, hateful to the nose, harmful to the brain, dangerous to the lungs.' These were the pompous words of which monarch, in his treatise expressing a distaste for tobacco? This monarch, born in 1566 in Edinburgh Castle, also saw himself as an expert on the practice of witchcraft in his published work *Daemonologie*. (Ahead of his time in some of his beliefs.) Married to Anne of Denmark, he approved a Bible in his name. Which king became the first monarch of both Scotland and England?

19

What word of four letters links: in politics, the singular form of the colloquial name of the oldest party in Canada (the Liberal Party); in psychology, the personality trait popularised by American academic Angela Duckworth in her book, subtitled *The Power of Passion and Perseverance*; and in geology, small loose particles of stone or sand?

20

With his father being the Poet Laureate of the UK between 1968 to 1972, which actor, who holds both British and Irish citizenship, is praised for his method acting? So devoted to his roles as to remain in character for the duration of a shoot, it's a good thing he's only starred in five films since 1998, or he'd be exhausted. Having announced his retirement in 2017, he has won three Oscar Academy Awards for Best Actor performances in *My Left Foot, There Will Be Blood* and *Lincoln*.

21

Formerly known as Travancore State, what state in India has been promoted for tourism as 'God's own country'? (Inhabitants of Yorkshire may beg to differ.) Its name originates from the word for 'coconut tree' in its native

language, Malayalam, and it became the first fully functionally-literate state in India in 1991. This state is renowned for its backwaters – no, literally: an interconnected network of canals, lakes and inlets.

22

'The best way to predict the future is to invent it.' These are the words of which Hungarian-British electrical engineer and physicist, most renowned for winning the 1971 Physics Nobel prize for his invention of holography?

23

What single-digit number links: in Judaism, the number of days of mourning after a funeral; in classics, the number 'Against Thebes' in an Aeschylus play; and in astronomy, the position of the planet Uranus in the order of orbital planets away from the sun?

24

'You can't change a regime on the basis of compassion. There's got to be something harder.' These are the words of which 1991 Nobel Laureate? Born in in Transvaal, South Africa in 1923, her novels include *The Conservationist, Burger's Daughter* and *July's People*. Renowned for her activism in the anti-apartheid movement, she died in 2014.

25

Answer as soon as you buzz! Identify the most common first name for US Presidents.

26

What decade links the following: the launch of Henry VIII's flagship *Mary Rose* at Portsmouth; the arrival of Spanish Conquistador Hernán Cortés in the Aztec court at Tenochtitlan; the death of Leonardo da Vinci, and the publication of the *95 Theses* by Martin Luther?

27

What part of the human body is connected by the following: the type of object being struck by Spanish gypsies in a chorus of Verdi's opera *Il Trovatore*; the nickname of King Edward I, which refers to his vow to avenge the rebellion of Robert Bruce, and a light frame or ring that holds the foot of a horse rider?

28

What three-word term has been defined as 'the sacrifice of realism and logic for the sake of enjoyment'? First phrased so in 1817 by poet Samuel Taylor Coleridge in his *Biographia Literaria*, Coleridge suggested that if a novelist could infuse a 'human interest and semblance of truth' into a tall tale, the reader may be able to temporarily halt judgment regarding the narrative's implausibility. Nowadays, the phrase is more often used to imply that the burden is on the reader or viewer.

29

'I stopped believing in Santa Claus when I was taken to see him in a department store and he asked for my autograph.' These are the words of which American actress, who remains the youngest recipient of an Oscar, receiving an Academy Juvenile Award at the age of six? Renowned for her mop of blonde curls and bright smile as a child, she was a US diplomat for the United Nations. She died in 2014.

30

What word of four letters links: a Hawaiian volcano goddess and creator; an active volcano on the surface of Jupiter's moon Io; and the Brazilian footballer born Edison Arantes do Nascimento?

•

CHAPTER 2:
20 SETS OF 3 BONUS QUESTIONS

For any correctly-answered Starter For 10 question, you win the chance to answer three – yes, THREE – bonus questions in this rapid-fire 'Bonus Question' section.

1

Three bonus questions on Summer Olympics host cities:

a

World War I caused the cancellation of the Berlin Games in which year?

b

Which General Secretary of the Central Committee of the Communist Party of the Soviet Union, from 1964 to 1982, opened the 1980 Moscow Games?

c

Who was the reigning British monarch at the time of London's first hosting the Games?

2

Three bonus questions on characters appearing on withdrawn UK bank notes:

a

This £10 note was replaced in 1994. Identify this person born in the city of the world-famous Uffizi Gallery, who used her passion for statistics (creating a 'coxcomb'; an intricate version of a pie chart) to save the lives of soldiers during the Crimean War?

b

This £5 note was withdrawn in 2003. Identify this person born in 1781, and renowned as the 'Father of the Railways'? (HINT: it was a man.)

c

This £50 note was withdrawn in 2014. Identify this person, who was the first Governor of the Bank of England from 1694 to 1697?

3

Three bonus questions on self-help books:

a

Born in 1946, which psychology professor at Stanford University is known for her work on the growth-versus-fixed mindset psychological traits?

b

What is the name of the book, published by Dale Carnegie in 1936, that is referred to in the 1968 film musical *Oliver!* by character Fagin, in his song 'Reviewing the Situation'?

c

Which English-born Canadian author is famed for his books *Tipping Point, Blink, Outliers, What the Dog Saw: And Other Adventures* and *David & Goliath*?

4

Three bonus questions on UK mathematicians and popularisers of the subject:

a

This lecturer in the Mathematics of Cities at

UCL gave a successful TED talk called 'The Mathematics of Love'? She regularly appears on radio and television, including as presenter of a biopic of Ada Lovelace, in the documentary *The Joy of Data* and in a BBC special, *Horizon: 10 Things You Need to Know About The Future*.

b

At the age of twenty-two, this Oxford Maths graduate replaced Carol Vorderman on Channel 4's letters and numbers gameshow *Countdown*. The numbers whizz now co-presents *Countdown* comedy spin-off *8 Out of 10 Cats Does Countdown*.

c

This popular science author's written works include *Fermat's Last Theorem, The Code Book* and *The Simpsons and Their Mathematical Secrets*. This author completed his PhD in particle physics at Emmanuel College Cambridge. Bobby is very proud about the author having gone to his current institution! His wife, Anita Anand, is the author of *Sophia*, a biography of the Indian princess and suffragette Sophia Duleep Singh.

5

Three bonus questions on fictional characters who went to Eton College:

a

This character is a recurring one in the Jeeves novels of British writer PG Wodehouse. As well as Eton, he was educated at Magdalen College, Oxford and is the first-person narrator of ten novels and over 30 short stories.

b

It is implied that this character attended Eton, as his final words are the school's motto *'Floreat Etona'*. This character is a pirate captain in a book alternatively known as *The Boy Who Wouldn't Grow Up*.

c

This iconic book and film character, conceived by Ian Fleming, briefly attended Eton aged '12 or thereabouts' but was removed after two terms because of mischief, going on to Fettes College in Scotland.

6

Three bonus questions on names of global financial institutions:

a

This American investment bank was founded in 1850. Its final Chief Executive Officer was Dick Fuld, who worked until the company filed for the largest bankruptcy in US history, on 15th September 2008.

b

This major American investment bank was founded in 1869 and is renowned for its list of former employees who have moved onto senior government positions; including former US Secretary of the Treasury Hank Paulson, European Central Bank President Mario Draghi and Governor of the Bank of England, Mark Carney.

c

This multinational bank was first established in Hong Kong in 1865 (and to a lesser extent in Shanghai) and has a dual primary listing in both Hong Kong and the London Stock Exchange. They brand themselves as the 'the world's local bank'.

7

Three bonus questions on British universities:

a

This university was founded in 1826 as London University by founders inspired by the ideas of utilitarian Jeremy Bentham. With the main campus around Gower Street, there is an ongoing myth that Jeremy Bentham's preserved body is brought out to preside over the university's council meetings.

b

Founded in 1582, this Scottish university is home to the UK's oldest student newspaper, called *The Student*, which was started in 1887 by Robert Louis Stevenson, author of *The Strange Case of Dr Jekyll and Mr Hyde*.

c

Part of the University of London, this particular university was founded in Egham, Surrey in 1879 and opened in 1886 by Queen Victoria as an all-female college. Their beautiful campus is renowned for the Founder's Building, a red-brick building modelled on the

Château de Chambord in the Loire Valley in France. The famous painting *The Two Princes Edward and Richard in the Tower, 1483* by Sir John Everett Millais is in this institution's collection.

8

Three bonus questions on saints:

a

Though not declared a saint by the Roman Catholic Church, this English mystic wrote *Revelations of Divine Love* around 1395. It is the first book in the English language known to have been written by a woman. Known for saying 'All shall be well, all shall be well and all manner of things shall be well', she is the subject of a 2016 written publication and a BBC documentary by Oxford cultural historian and broadcaster Dr Janina Ramirez.

b

This saint, renowned for his love of a minimalist lifestyle, founded a religious order in his name in the early

13th century. He has been associated with the patronage of animals and the natural environment. The current Pope, born Jorge Mario Bergoglio, has taken on this saint's name.

c

This saint was born in central Italy in 1221 and named John. He received the name for which he is better known after St Francis of Assisi prayed for John's recovery from a dangerous illness. Young John supposedly cried out 'good fortune', which is a rough translation of his name as a saint.

9

Three bonus questions on birds in fiction:

a

Long John Silver, the main villain in Robert Louis Stevenson's 1883 novel *Treasure Island*, has contributed to the image of the pirate in popular culture. The pirate is renowned for his peg-leg and his parrot, who is often seen sitting on his shoulder. What is the parrot's name?

b

Published by the American Richard Bach in 1970, this novella is about a bird learning about life and flight, and is a homily to self-perfection. This bird seeks to escape the monotony of the *wake up, eat fish, sleep* routine of regular seagulls. American science fiction author Ray Bradbury says that the author does two things with the book for which he is 'deeply grateful': 'He gives me flight, he makes me young'.

c

This parrot sidekick of the main villain Jafar from Disney's 1992 animated film *Aladdin* is often causing mischief. Despite sharing his name with one of Shakespeare's most iconic antagonists, from *Othello*, the parrot's character is apparently an homage to an identically-named red parrot from a *Tintin* adventure.

10

Three bonus questions on West Ham United:

a

What year was the club founded? It shares this year with the Dreyfus Affair in France, the first year of Oscar Wilde's two-year imprisonment, and the death of Friedrich Engels.

b

West Ham fans often enjoy claiming that they won the football FIFA World Cup in 1966 as their player Bobby Moore captained the winning England side and their players provided all of England's four goals. Geoff Hurst is renowned for his hat trick, but which other West Ham player also scored in the final?

c

West Ham have moved from their 1904 historical ground in the Upton Park area to the Olympic Stadium in Stratford in 2016. What was the official name of their old ground?
It shares this name with the surname of the second wife of Henry VIII, who is believed to have stayed at or owned a house that the club rented in the area.

11
Three questions on personalities from the fitness industry:

a

Having studied Sports Science at St Mary's University Twickenham, this British fitness Internet and TV star shot to fame through his YouTube channel and show *The Body Coach*. His cookbook *Lean in 15: 15-Minute Meals* was a top selling book in 2015. Who, in 2017, broke a Guinness World Record by leading the largest ever high-intensity interval training class with 3,804 participants?

b

One of the leading proponents of the high-intensity fitness market is this American fitness trainer and motivational speaker. Renowned for *T25, Insanity* and *Hip-Hop Abs*, which star of the Beachbody brand often asks his viewers to 'come on y'all', 'dig deeper' and to 'trust and believe'?

c

Which Jamaican-born British fitness instructor rose to fame in the early 1990s through appearances on the UK breakfast TV show *GMTV* (often performing before *Power Rangers*)? He would often perform workout sessions live, gaining attention for his extremely tight-fitting and highly colourful Spandex outfits.

12

Three bonuses on British public figures of South Asian ancestry who have studied Economics at university:

a

This graduate of Oxford's Philosophy, Politics & Economics (PPE) course is an actor and rapper who initially came to prominence in the UK in the 2010 comedy *Four Lions*. His breakout role was in 2014 thriller film *Nightcrawler* starring Jake Gyllenhaal and he has subsequently starred in *Star Wars: Rogue One* and HBO miniseries *The Night Of* (for which he won an Emmy). Some viewers may have seen him duel against Monkman & Seagull in a *University Challenge*-style mini-match on the BBC's *The One Show*.

b

This politician also studied PPE at Oxford. She began her career as a research assistant to Michael Young, the man who coined the term 'meritocracy' and set the vision for the creation of the Open University. She worked as an Associate Director of the Young Foundation, a think tank focused on social innovation, and went on to co-found UpRising, a charity that promotes youth leadership development programmes. In 2010, she was elected as an MP for Bethnal Green & Bow for Labour, replacing George Galloway from the Respect party.

c

This Cambridge Economics graduate and television presenter was most renowned for being the longest-serving female presenter of the children's TV programme *Blue Peter*. Indeed, she was voted as the nation's favourite Blue Peter presenter in a poll of *Radio Times* readers. She has also co-written, with her husband the satirist Charlie Brooker, an episode of Channel 4's anthology series *Black Mirror*. Her sister Rupa was elected MP for Ealing Central and Acton at the 2015 General Election.

13

Three bonus questions on boroughs of London:

a

This is the most northern borough of London. First recorded in the Domesday Book in 1084, the translation from the Old English is either 'open land of a man called Ēana' or 'where lambs are reared'. Famous people born in this borough include singer Amy Winehouse; creator of a sewer network for central London Sir Joseph Bazalgette; and entertainer Sir Bruce Forsyth.

b

This borough's name is a portmanteau of two of its former Essex county boroughs. This borough famously contains most of the Olympic Park, the historic street market 'Queen's Market' and London City Airport. Esteemed persons born in this borough include the 'Forces' Sweetheart' Dame Vera Lynn; Victorian poet and inventor of sprung rhythm Gerard Manley Hopkins; and the bird-named author of this quiz book.

c

This borough hosts the Wimbledon tennis championships each summer. Renowned people born here include author of *The Good Solider*, Ford Madox Ford; actor Oliver Reed, known for his heavy drinking, sometimes live on TV; and finally classicist and poet Robert Graves, known for historical novels such as *I, Claudius.*

14

Three bonus questions on Nordic popular music:

a

This Icelandic singer has had several top 10 hits in the UK including 'It's Oh So Quiet' and 'Army Of Me'. She won the Best Actress Award at the 2000 Cannes Film Festival for her role in the film *Dancer in the Dark*. In 2015, the Museum of Modern Art in New York held a full-scale retrospective dedicated to this musician.

b

Hailing from Norway and only born in 1996, this Norwegian singer achieved international success in 2017 with her single 'Don't Kill My Vibe'. Having performed on Park Stage at Glastonbury, *The Guardian* newspaper suggested that she may be worthy of headlining the festival in the future. Her name derives from a word in Old Norse meaning 'victory'.

c

This Swedish pop group formed in 1972 and their band's name is derived from the initials of their first names. Having won the Eurovision song contest in 1974 with a song referring to Napoleon's surrender at an 1815 battle, they inspired a musical that became the fastest-selling DVD of all time in the UK.

15

Three bonuses on the UK education system:

a

Broadly equivalent to the American Ivy League, what name is given to the self-selecting association of twenty-four public research universities in the UK? Established in 1994, the group's name is derived from its first informal meetings, in a particular hotel named for the Bloomsbury Square it was located in.

b

During the Second World War, the 1944 Education Act was authored by this Conservative minister. It defined the split between primary and secondary education at age 11 that has since become usual. This minister held the posts of deputy Prime Minister, Chancellor and Home Secretary. The 'post-war consensus' is sometimes described as 'Butskellism', an elision of this politician's name with that of his Labour counterpart Hugh Gaitskell.

c

Chief inspectors of this non-ministerial department of the UK government include Sir Chris Woodhead, Sir Mike Tomlinson, Sir David Bell, Christine Gilbert and Sir Michael Wilshaw. This body is responsible for conducting inspections of a range of educational institutions.

16

Three questions on newly-named elements in the periodic table, named in 2016. Elements can be named to reflect a mythological concept, a mineral, a place/country, a property or a scientist:

a

Element number 113 was discovered at the RIKEN Nishina Center for Accelerator-Based Science in Japan. Its name comes from the common Japanese name for Japan.

b

Element number 115 was first synthesised in 2003 by a team of Russian and American scientists at the Joint Institute for Nuclear Research in Dubna, Russia. It is named for the city region in which the JINR is situated.

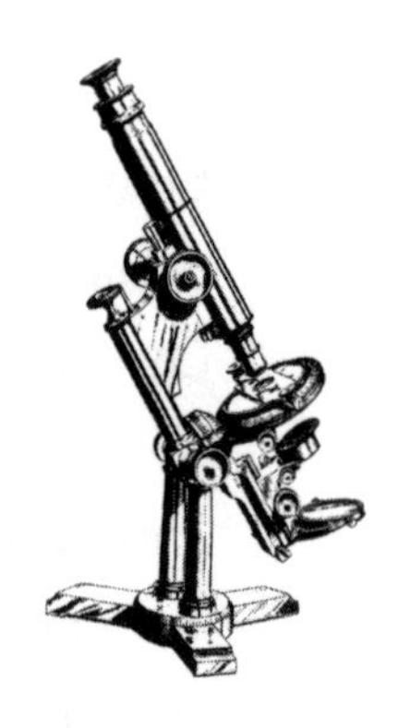

c

Element number 117 is currently the second-heaviest known element. Its discovery was officially announced in Dubna, Russia in 2010. It is named after a state in the USA with the nickname of The Volunteer State, the capital of which is Nashville. Contributions towards the discovery were made by the Oak Ridge National Laboratory and Vanderbilt Laboratory, in the American state.

17

Three bonuses on UK children's laureates. This two-year post developed following a discussion between then-Poet Laureate, Ted Hughes, and a famous children's author:

a

This man was the third holder of the post, between 2003-05. He is best known for his 1982 children's novel *War Horse,* which was adapted into a stage play and a successful Stephen Spielberg film. His wife, Clare, is the eldest daughter of Sir Allen Lane, the founder of Penguin Books.

b

This fourth holder of the post, between 2005-07, writes children's novels that frequently feature themes of adoption, divorce and mental illness. She lives in a Victorian villa along with a personal library of 15,000 books.

Her *Tracey Beaker* series has been adapted into four television series.

c

This eighth holder of the post, between 2013-15, mainly writes literature and television drama for children and young adults. Born in London to parents from Barbados, her popularly acclaimed series *Noughts and Crosses* uses a fictional dystopia setting to explore love, racism and violence. She has written television scripts for episodes of children's drama *Byker Grove* and had television adaptations made of her novels *Whizziwhig* and *Pig-Heart Boy*.

18

Three bonus questions on billionaires who have made their wealth through online businesses:

a

This American technology and retail entrepreneur is best known as the founder and boss of the world's largest online retailer, Amazon. Other ventures include the founding of 'Blue Origin' with test flights to space and plans for suborbital human spaceflight. In July 2017, he was briefly the richest person in the world. No need to pity him for losing the top spot since.

b

This Chinese business magnate is the founder and executive chairman of Alibaba Group, a collection of Internet-based enterprises. He used to practice English daily by talking to English speakers at an international hotel, a seventy-minute bike ride from his house. Despite being rejected by both KFC and Harvard for positions, he is regularly near the top of the list of Asia's wealthiest men.

c

Born in Paris to Iranian parents, this entrepreneur moved to the United States as a child. He is the founder of the online auction site eBay. Since 2010, he has been involved in online journalism as the head of investigative reporting at news website 'Honolulu Civil Beat'.

19

Three bonus questions on dinosaurs:

a

Born in Lancaster in 1804, this biologist's campaign for natural specimens in the British Museum to be given a new home resulted in the 1881 establishment of the Natural History Museum in South Kensington, London. He is remembered for coining the word 'dinosauria', meaning 'terrible lizard' – a terrible definition.

b

A major shake-up of dinosaur theory, where dinosaurs may have first emerged 15 million years earlier than previously believed, was published in March 2017 in this English multidisciplinary scientific journal by Cambridge researchers led by Dr Matthew Baron. Name this journal; first published in 1869, which published landmark papers such as proof of the existence of the neutron by Chadwick in 1932 and Watson & Crick's structure of DNA in 1953.

c

The last of the non-avian dinosaurs were believed to have become extinct about 65 million years ago. In the 1980s, father and son scientists Luis and Walter Alvarez discovered a distinct layer of which periodic table element, found in abundance in space at a time that corresponds to the time which dinosaurs died out, suggesting an asteroid or meteor hit Earth at this time? This element has atomic number 77 and a meaning 'of rainbows' from its Latin origins, because its salts are strongly coloured.

20

Three bonuses on the Russian composer and conductor Sergei Rachmaninov:

a

This English rock band was formed in Teignmouth, Devon in 1994. Lead singer Matt Bellamy has cited the influence of the Russian composer on some of the band's songs such as 'Space Dementia' and 'Butterflies and Hurricanes' and has even played segments of Rachmaninov during concerts.

b

Rachmaninov composed a rhapsody on a theme named after this Italian violinist, regarded as one of the most celebrated violin virtuoso of all time. This rhapsody is a set of twenty-four variations on the 24th and last of the violin caprices composed by this violinist. In Don Nigro's satirical comedy drama of 1995 also named after the violinist, the violinist sells his soul to the Devil. Name the violinist.

c

In 1997, Geoffrey Rush was awarded an Oscar, the Academy Award for Best Actor, depicting the role of pianist David Helfgott who suffered a mental breakdown. In the film, David enters a concerto competition and chooses to play Rachmaninov's demanding 3rd concerto.

CATEGORIES OF QUESTIONS

10 or more questions on a single category or theme. You can come to these from the 'Starter for 10s'.

SPORTS

Bobby pushed hard to include 100 questions on his beloved West Ham United football club within this section, but sadly (sensibly) Eric vetoed this decision. The compromise was 30 general sports questions, in which Eric could focus on language.

Eric enjoys working out in the gym, but Bobby is a sports fanatic. Bobby is one of the few people who can claim to have played football on the same pitch (at different times) with sporting and footballing royalty (and does; often). Bobby actually played against England international striker Jermain Defoe at primary school level (Jermain also went to the same secondary school, St Bonaventure's in East London, as Bobby). After winning a Sixth Form scholarship to study at Eton College, Bobby played against Prince Harry in the inter-house football competition.

Bobby is a fan of High Intensity Interval Training: a form of exercise which reduces the participant to a sweaty heap while increasing their fitness (and endurance of pain). In particular, he is a devotee of US instructor of

'Insanity' fitness, Sean T., and British 'Body Coach' Joe Wicks. He enjoys middle-distance running too. When in East London, he runs with his purple-clad East End Road Runners, and when in Cambridge, with the 'Cambridge University Hare & Hounds'.

CHAPTER 3:
10 WORDS IN THE NAMES OF BRITISH FOOTBALL CLUBS

Each answer is also (roughly) a word that appears in the name of a British football club. Eric knows almost nothing about the teams themselves, so this is as close as he could get to a sports category.

1

The word for one of these facilities comes from an Arabic word for a workshop. Dante compares the condition of one of these facilities, located in Venice, to an aspect of the Inferno. The Venetian facility was used to construct and repair ships and produce other naval goods. Later, Franklin Delano Roosevelt called on Americans to become a metaphorical one of what kind of facility on behalf of democracy?

2

A predecessor of Chiquita Brands International was a fruit company with this word in its name. Varney Air Lines, an early American air transportation company, would merge with other companies to form an airline with this word in its name. What word appears in the name of a Middle Eastern nation, a sovereign state located on the majority of an archipelago off the northern coast of Europe, and a country in North America?

3

In the ancient Roman Empire, these structures came in *rustica* and *urbana* varieties. During the Renaissance, architects such as Palladio studied one of these structures that had belonged to Emperor Hadrian. Notable examples of these structures that were built during the Renaissance include one named for Cardinal Farnese, one named after Cardinal d'Este and several named after the Medici. What word for a structure once referred only to country estates, but now can be used to refer to urban residences as well?

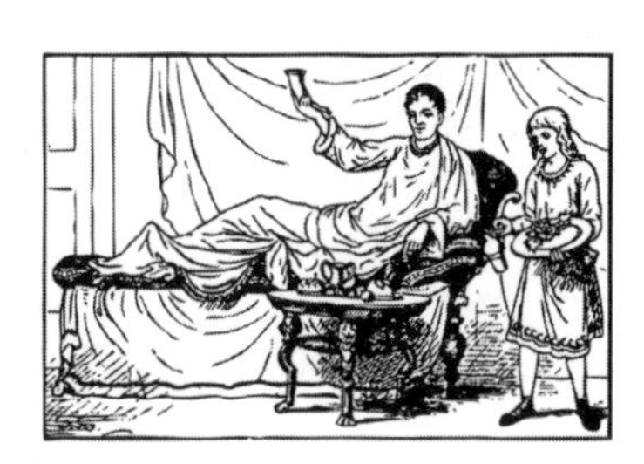

4

A poem in the Exeter book was given this name by Anglo-Saxon scholar Benjamin Thorpe. The poem describes the plight of a warrior who has lost his lord and now lives as a homeless exile, reminiscing over happier days past. What name is also used by several football clubs, one of which has grounds at Molineux Stadium and another at Macron Stadium?

5

In Elizabethan times, Francis Drake landed on the west coast of North America, giving rise to a claim for territory called 'Nova' followed by this word. A character with this name appears in a poem called 'Jerusalem' by William Blake (but not the same 'Jerusalem' poem that is used in the song). What word is often preceded by the adjective 'perfidious' in a pejorative term?

6

Francis of Assisi became one of these in 1228 and Thomas à Becket became one of these in 1173. Joan of Arc became one of these in 1920. What did John XXIII and John Paul II become in 2014?

7

The Canadian Armed Forces includes patrol groups that use this name. These groups are tasked with patrolling remote areas. The United States Army includes a regiment with this word in its name. The regiment operates as an airborne raiding force. What name is also used by a division within the Texas Department of Public Safety, tasked with conducting investigations, assisting local law enforcement and protecting elected officials?

8

This building inspired the construction of similar buildings in Montreal, Munich, and New York. After serving its initial purpose, this building was moved to a park that still now contains sculptures of dinosaurs, though the building of which we speak was destroyed in a fire in 1936. What building was constructed in Hyde Park to house the thrilling-sounding Great Exhibition of the Works of Industry of All Nations, held in 1851?

9

This military commander was given his nickname by his Scottish enemies, because he was constantly seeking and preparing for battle. A descendant of Henry III, this man was knighted by Edward III at age fourteen. He appears as a character in Shakespeare's *Henry IV: Part 1*, where he is made young enough to be a rival to Prince Hal (he was actually considerably older, but the bard knew what hooks a crowd). What man died at the Battle of Shrewsbury while taking part in a rebellion against Henry IV?

10

This day of the week is named after a god who was considered to be the German equivalent of Mercury. If the first day in the Biblical creation narrative was a Sunday, then God created the Sun, the Moon and the stars on this day of the week. On what day of the week are Prime Minister's Questions traditionally held in the United Kingdom (as of 2017)?

•

CHAPTER 4: 20 SPORTS TIME!

A category about sports in general.

1

Sun cream and scarves. Shorts and ear warmers. Sleeveless vests and thick ski jackets. Hosting a Summer Olympic Games and a Winter Olympic Games in theory requires two wildly different climactic environments for the host city. However, which city will attempt to defy the meteorological gods by becoming the first to have hosted both the Summer and Winter Games? This city is due to host the Winter Olympics 2022 to complete their pair.

2

'I am the master of my fate: I am the captain of my soul'. These are the closing lines of which short Victorian poem published by William Ernest Henley in 1875? Initially untitled, its title (Latin for 'unconquered') was added by the editor Arthur Quiller-Couch. The poem is also the name of a 2009 sports drama film directed by Clint Eastwood, starring Morgan Freeman as Nelson Mandela and Matt Damon as the

Springboks captain Francois Pienaar. The film follows the events in South Africa before and during their 1995 Rugby World Cup triumph.

3

Fulham Football Club, Crabtree Tavern, Harrods Furniture Depository, the Hammersmith Bridge, St Paul's School, Fuller's Brewery, Chiswick Pier, The Bandstand and Barnes Railway Bridge. These are some of the landmarks between Mortlake and Putney for which annual event?

4

2 hours 55 minutes in 1908, 2 hours 29 minutes in 1925, 2 hours 18 minutes in 1953, 2 hours 10 minutes in 1967...the men's marathon world record is slowly inching towards the fantastical sub-2-hour time. In May 2017, Kenya's Eliud Kipchoge completed the marathon on the Formula One racing track at Monza Italy in a time just 25 seconds outside the 2 hour barrier. Which sports brand sponsored this attempt?

5

The song 'Barcelona' featured heavily in the 1992 Summer Olympics in Barcelona. The Spanish parts were sung by operatic soprano Montserrat Caballé and the English lyrics were sung by which other British vocalist?

6

This person was inspired to take up her sport by reading Arthur Ransome's *Swallows and Amazons* series of books. She taught herself to sew on a piece of pigskin, so as to be prepared to sew her tongue back on in the event of an accident on a boat! Despite growing up in a landlocked part of England's north, which English yachtswoman broke the world record in 2005 for the fastest solo voyage around the globe?

7

Brazilian football icon Pelé said that West Ham United and England hero Bobby Moore was the greatest defender he had ever played against. However these two men were on the same team, alongside other stars such as Spurs' Ossie Ardiles, in which 1981 film about Allied prisoners of war who play an exhibition football match against a German team? England goalkeeping legend Gordon Banks (renowned for his miracle save against Pelé in the 1970 World Cup) coached Rocky (sorry – Sylvester Stallone) for the film.

8

At Oxford University's Iffley Road Track, Sir Roger Bannister became the first person to run a sub-four minute mile with 3:59.4 on 6th May 1954. However, which Australian runner broke this world record six weeks later on June 21st with 3:58.0? They then competed in 'The Race of the Century' at the 1954 British Empire Games on August 7th, listened to by 100 million people on the radio. The moment Bannister won as the Australian looked over his left shoulder on the final turn was immortalised by a bronze sculpture of this moment in Vancouver.

9

A pleasant village green on a Sunday afternoon with scones and jam laid on for tea – the archetypal setting of the English cricket match. This classic view of the 'gentleman's game' was echoed in a scene from Danny Boyle's opening ceremony, with cricket being played in the London 2012 Olympic stadium. However, which two teams (not including England, surprisingly) contested not just the first official international cricket match, but the first international game of any sport in 1844?

10

'The Baltimore Bullet', Michael Phelps, is the most decorated Olympian of all time, with 28 medals (including 23 swimming gold medals). In an echo of runner Jesse Owens' race against a horse in 1945, what creature known scientifically as *Carcharodon carcharias* did Phelps take on in July 2017? With Michael wearing a wetsuit and a monofin, the Discovery Channel somewhat disappointingly used a computer-generated version of this creature in the race.

11

One of the greatest baseball players of all time, Joe DiMaggio played for his entire 13 year career for the New York Yankees. Despite apparently not wanting to meet DiMaggio as she feared he was a stereotypical arrogant sportsman, which American actress, born Norma Jeane Mortensen, eventually married him in 1954? After her tragic death in 1962, Joe showed his devotion to her by delivering a half-dozen red roses three times a week to her crypt for 20 years. What a charmer.

12

Children's BBC TV presenter and Wigan's favourite puppet, Hacker T. Dog, is a fan of both of our quiz authors, tweeting: 'Monkman and Seagull are my heroes, and I don't care who knows it. That is all!' However he is even fonder of which sports TV presenter? Reaching a career-high singles ranking of World No. 3 and winning the 1976 French Open, this woman is a mainstay of the two weeks of the Wimbledon tennis coverage.

13

Last achieved in the 1992 Barcelona Olympics, this feat has become virtually impossible to achieve in its field of sport. The first man to manage it was Alexander Dityatin at the 1980 games; and Mary Lou Retton in 1984 also did it. Despite the scoreboard causing confusion as it only allowed three digits, in the 1976 Montreal Olympics what did 14-year-old Romanian gymnast Nadia Comăneci achieve?

14

Innocent Moves is the UK title of a 1993 American drama starring actors Ben Kingsley and Laurence Fishburne in a biopic of chess prodigy, Josh Waitzkin. However, the film's title in America is *Searching For* [...], with the name of a different American chess player following. Which player is this? *Pawn Sacrifice* showed actor Toby Maguire star as this chess player, in a film which culminated in this player's iconic 1972 World Chess Championship against Boris Spassky in Reyjkjavik, Iceland.

15

For those who have played a round of golf (Center Parcs mini-golf doesn't count), they will be used to 'bogeys' (scores of one over par on a hole, nothing to do with dried nasal mucus). With a 'birdie' and 'eagle' representing one and two under par respectively, what large bird of the family *diomedidae* is used to signify a rare three under par? It is the same bird shot by the mariner in Samuel Taylor Coleridge's poem 'The Rime of the Ancient Mariner'.

16

'Winning isn't everything; it's the only thing'. This quotation is widely, but wrongly originally attributed to Vince Lombardi, arguably the greatest American football coach ever, and the man for whom the National Football League's top trophy is named. However, which UCLA Bruins football coach originally said this? He shares a surname with another American legend, the Colonel best known for founding the fast food chicken restaurant chain KFC.

17

With a record 23 Grand Slam singles tennis titles, Serena Williams is not only one of the greatest sportspersons of all time but also is name-checked in the lyrics of a song by Justin Timberlake (Bobby once sang a line from a Snoop Dogg rap, loudly and unashamedly, while attending Wimbledon, watching the Williams sisters in a doubles match). Serena recently took time off from tennis to have her first child, baby girl Alexis Olympia Ohanian, Jr with Alexis Ohanian. Set up in 2005, Alexis is the co-founder of which American social news and media aggregation website?

18

With a leap of 8.90m that smashed the previous world record by 55cm (!), Bob Beamon held the long jump world record for 23 years; from the 1968 Mexico City Olympics until the 1991 Tokyo World Championships. At the aforementioned World Championships in Tokyo (one of the greatest sporting contests of all time, to rival the Monkman vs. Seagull *University Challenge* 2017 semi-final), the 8.90m was twice bettered by which two long jumpers? One achieved a wind-assisted 8.91m and the other 8.95m, still a world record to this day.

19

The Wall Game, where there has not been a goal scored in the annual fixture on St Andrew's Day since 1909. The Field Game, where there are two versions of offside (horizontal and lateral). Fives, a handball game developed from the side of a school's chapel. 'The Battle of Waterloo was won on the playing fields' of what school? Note that this quote attributed to Wellington was probably apocryphal.

20

As of 2017, the Indian Hindi-language film *Dangal* was the top selling film of all time at the Indian box office. The film, co-produced by Disney, follows the struggle and success of an Indian father and his two daughters, who he trains to win wrestling medals at the 2010 Commonwealth Games. What is the name of the film's producer who also starred as the father? He shares his name (albeit first name spelt slightly differently) with the Bolton-born British boxer who became Team GB's youngest boxing Olympic medallist at age 17 in 2004 and was a former light-welterweight world champion.

ARTS AND HUMANITIES

Bobby and Eric are art connoisseurs, even if they occasionally might find it hard to keep their van Dykes and van Eycks straight.

CHAPTER 5: 10 RED, YELLOW AND BLUE – THE ARTS

Bobby was asked to write an article for Art UK, a charity with the purpose of creating a complete record of the national collection of paintings. His chosen topic: 'How to answer every art question on University Challenge*'. Whilst this is no small challenge, both Bobby and Eric do encourage readers to become amateur connoisseurs: enjoy art in the first instance, and the knowledge will follow. https://artuk.org/discover/stories/how-to-answer-every-art-question-on-university-challenge#*

1

The Equestrian Statue of Gattamelata at Padua, the sculpture *The Pietà* in St Peter's Basilica, *Lady with Ermine*, the fresco *The School of Athens* in the Apostolic Palace. These are all works by four Italian Renaissance artists who are linked by sharing their first names with four fictional anthropomorphic reptiles of the order *Testudines*. Which group links these artists and for an extra point, what are their names?

2

2014's *Dawn of the Planet of the Apes*, the 2014 *Godzilla*, 2013's *Pacific Rim* and 2006's *X-Men: The Last Stand*. These four films are connected through all featuring which famous architectural structure? Engineered by Joseph B. Strauss and Charles Ellis, this structure was opened in 1937. It connects Marin County to the city of San Francisco. The structure's signature colour of 'International Orange' was meant to have been temporary but is now iconic.

3

Mahatma Gandhi and Jesus Christ didn't make the cut. Psychiatrist Carl Jung, writer Edgar Allan Poe, dancer Fred Astaire, politician Sir Robert Peel, actress Marilyn Monroe, philosopher Karl Marx and writer Oscar Wilde were chosen, however. Also joining in are a doll of the Hindu goddess Lakshmi, a stone figure of Snow White and a garden gnome. Created by pop artists Jann Haworth and Peter Blake, what iconic album cover of 1967 is this?

4

'I don't think there's an illustrator who's as good as a Titian or a Rembrandt... but then, Rembrandt was a bit of an illustrator on the quiet, you know?' These are the words of which illustrator, born in 1932 in Kent, who always wears white plimsolls (canvas sneakers for our American friends)? Having written and illustrated *Zagazoo* and *Mister Magnolia*, he is best-known for his illustrations of books by Roald Dahl.

5

Argentine Marxist revolutionary Che Guevara was in Havana, Cuba for a memorial service for the victims of the explosion of *La Coubre*, a French freighter which blew up while unloading munitions in Havana harbour. Who took the iconic photo of Che since named 'Heroic Guerrilla Fighter' at this service? The Victoria and Albert Museum have claimed that this has been reproduced more than any other image in photography.

6

Carried out by two men posing as police officers in the early hours of 18th March 1990, the highest-value theft of private property ever took place at the Isabella Stewart Gardner Museum in Boston. Who is the Dutch artist of what is considered the most valuable unrecovered painting? Worth $200 million, *The Concert* is one of only 34 paintings universally attributed to this artist and in an episode of *The Simpsons*, this artwork is shown in Mr Burns' stolen artwork collection.

7

8,000 soldiers, 130 chariots with 520 horses, 150 cavalry horses. Dating from the third century BC and discovered in 1974 by local farmers in Shaanxi province in China, what is the name for this collection of earthenware sculptures? The 2007 exhibition in the British Museum which showed a fraction of this collection was the museum's second most successful exhibition ever. (After the 1972 Tutankhamun craze!)

8

'If you seek his memorial, look about you.' These are the words on the gravestone of which architect and co-founder of the Royal Society, who died in 1723? He was responsible for rebuilding 52 churches (one for every week of the year) in the City of London after the Great Fire in 1666. (He might be disappointed by the materialism and lack of spirituality there today). As well as designing the chapel at Emmanuel College, Cambridge (Bobby will show you around if you ask nicely), his works include the Royal Observatory at Greenwich and the façade of Hampton Court Palace.

9

'I think it would blow the imagination of the Romans if they could see it and it would certainly boggle the mind of Gustave Eiffel if he could see it. The more you look at it, the more it sticks in your mind.' Standing at 114.5 metres tall and designed by Sir Anish Kapoor and Cecil Balmond, what is Boris Johnson describing? This sculpture and observation tower is in Bobby's proverbial back yard in the Olympic Park in Stratford.

10

A long, meandering earthquake-style crack; over 100 million porcelain sunflower seeds; 14,000 translucent white polyethylene boxes stacked in various ways; and a fine mist in the air with a circular disc made up of 100s of monochromatic lamps. These were all temporary works which have been exhibited in which hall of the Tate Modern museum which once housed the electricity generators of the old power station? It shares its name with a rotary mechanical device that draws energy from fluid flow.

CHAPTER 6: 10 LITERATURE

A classic category: good old books.

1

This humourist studied economics with Thorstein Veblen and became a professor at McGill University. He found greater success as a writer than as a professor. Later in life, he described himself as a "professor emeritus", where e- means "out" and "meritus" means "ought to be".' His short story 'Self-Made Men' describes two wealthy businessmen who boast about the deprivations they suffered earlier in life. What Anglo-Canadian author created the fictional Canadian town of Mariposa?

2

This author once ghost-wrote a short story for Harry Houdini, recounting how the magician allegedly escaped from an Egyptian pyramid. This author also wrote several short stories set in the 'Dreamlands', as well as an essay arguing for the superiority of cats over dogs – a most pressing academic argument. What author also created a 'mythos' that includes such beings as the shoggoths, Nyarlathotep and Cthulhu?

3

This play contains what some consider to be an early description of Gresham's law. The play, a comedy, includes a competition between two tragic playwrights. Much of the action takes place in Hades. The play won first prize at the Lenaia festival held in 405 BC. Which play by Aristophanes contains a chorus sung by the animals that are its namesake?

4

The main character in this book can recite the Bible by heart – a useful skill for impressing people. Throughout the story, the main character takes on many different roles, including those of a tutor, a seminary student, a secretary, a secret messenger and an army officer. He also engages in two love affairs, one with the wife of a mayor and the other with the daughter of a marquis. Which novel by Stendhal has a title that is taken to refer to the clergy and the military?

5

The author of this novel uses Early Modern English to denote dialogue that occurs in other languages. One character in this novel, Hurree Chunder Mookerjee, describes himself as 'good enough Herbert Spencerian'. A real-life spy got his nickname from the title character of this novel. What novel by Rudyard Kipling describes the story of a child who is variously a spy for the British Raj and a disciple of a Buddhist monk?

6

This amorous character appears in a 17th-century play by the Spanish monk Tirso de Molina. In Molina's play, this character is killed by the ghost of a man he murdered. This character meets a similar fate in a 19th-century play by José Zorilla, however, in this version, not authored by a monk, the love of the blameless Doña Inés allows him into heaven. What character is the title character of an opera with a libretto written by Lorenzo da Ponte and music written by Wolfgang Amadeus Mozart?

7

This poet, story-writer and artist wrote the lyrics to two national anthems (HINT: Enoch Sontonga is not the answer to this question). He was knighted, but he renounced his knighthood following the Jallianwala Bagh massacre. This poet wrote an essay criticising Mohandas Karamchand Gandhi's exhortation to Indians to use charkha spinning wheels. What poet is famous for writing the *Gitanjali* or *Song Offerings*?

8

This narrative describes a method for hunting what are likely crocodiles or alligators in which spikes are hidden in sand that pierce the beasts as they drag themselves to the shore. The narrative is written in Old French, even though its authors were from Pisa and Venice. The veracity of what narrative has been questioned, in part because it does not mention chopsticks, tea or Chinese characters in its descriptions of China of the time?

9

In one story by this macabre author, the protagonist and narrator is rescued by General Lasalle, one of Napoleon's generals. Another of this author's protagonist/narrators has the family motto *'Nemo Me Impune Lacessit'*. The relative success of one of this author's poems compared to one of his short stories led him to write 'The bird beat the bug'. What American author wrote the poem 'Ulalume', containing the lines 'As the lavas that restlessly roll / Their sulphurous currents down Yaanek / In the ultimate climes of the pole'?

10

One author of this name served as a naval officer and wrote historical fiction about the American Revolutionary War and the American Civil War. Another author of this name served as a cavalry officer and wrote a novel about a revolution in a fictional European country (he is more famous for other accomplishments in the political field, though). Which name was shared by two authors, one of whom wrote a letter to the other in which he offered to use a middle initial in his publications to avoid confusion?

CHAPTER 7: 10 ENGLISH WORDS OF NON-INDO-EUROPEAN ORIGIN

English is an Indo-European language, so most of its words naturally have Indo-European roots. Some come from the Germanic languages from which English developed. Others come from Latin and its daughter tongues, whose words came into English over centuries of dialogue with the continent. Not a small number come from Greek, especially words relating to religion or science.

This category is for those rare English words that come from non-Indo-European languages.

1

The word used to describe this substance comes from Quechua, the language of the Inca Empire. It means 'dung' in that language – because dung is what it is. However, it was highly valued: pursuit of this substance, used as a fertiliser, led the United States to authorise the acquisition of outlying islands and it also led to a war between Spain and some of its former colonies in South America. It led the Pacific island nation of Nauru to become very rich, at least until it ran out... What is this substance?

2

The word for this profession comes from the languages of the Tungusic peoples. The word

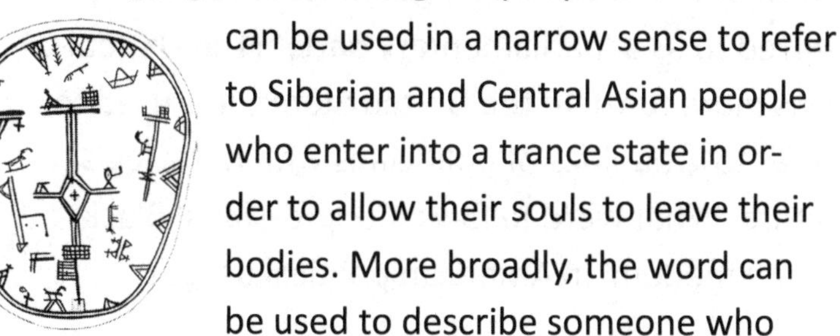

can be used in a narrow sense to refer to Siberian and Central Asian people who enter into a trance state in order to allow their souls to leave their bodies. More broadly, the word can be used to describe someone who communicates with spirits on behalf of others. What is the profession described here?

3

The word for this reptile comes from Zulu or Swahili. There are actually four species which bear this name, three of which are green and one which is called black, though individuals tend to be grey or brown. All varieties of this reptile are venomous, the black variety extremely so. What is the name of snakes in the genus *dendroapsis*?

4

The word may come from an Algonkian word meaning 'advisor'. In Canada, the Australian Labor Party and in several other Commonwealth countries, the word is used to refer to what in the United Kingdom would be referred to as a 'parliamentary party' (The UK really is more fun!). In the United States, it is used to refer to groupings of politicians within the legislature. What word follows 'Congressional Black' and 'Freedom' in American political usage?

5

This group of birds get their name from a Nahuatl (Aztec) word that refers to the bird's tail feathers. The name of what group of birds also appears in the name of an Aztec deity and is also the name of the currency of Guatemala?

6

The word used to describe this facility is one of the few words in the English language borrowed from Finnish. The facility is very popular in Finland; many houses have one, as does the Finnish

Parliament. What facility operates by heating rocks on a wood or electric stove and then creating steam by pouring or sprinkling water onto the rocks?

7

The word for this action comes from Chinese words for 'touch' and 'head'. Traditionally, someone performing this action would prostrate him- or herself and touch the ground with his or her head. What word is today used to denote acts of subservience?

8

This word comes from Malay. Spelled one way, it appears in the title of a self-referential, fourth-wall-breaking cartoon in which Daffy Duck is tormented by the animator, who is revealed to be Bugs Bunny. Spelled a different way, it appears in the title of an episode of the original series of *Star Trek*. If you've seen both recently, you must be a well-rounded individual. What word means 'a frenzied attack'? In English, it usually follows the word 'run'.

9

The word comes from Polynesian languages. Originally, that word may have referred to natural phenomena, such as lightning or storms. It eventually came to mean a supernatural 'power' or 'effectiveness'. What word is used in English to refer to a unit of magical energy, especially in roleplaying games and in *Magic: The Gathering*?

10

This prefix may come from an Akkadian word meaning 'gold'. It comes to English through Greek. It is used in the word for a flower that is popular in China and appears on the Imperial Seal of Japan. It is also used in the nickname of a Byzantine preacher named John, deriving from his eloquent speech. What prefix is used in the name of the pupal phase of butterflies?

•

CHAPTER 8: 10 NAMES OF BOOKS IN THE OLD TESTAMENT OF THE BIBLE

Every answer in this category is also (roughly) the name of a book in the Old Testament of the Bible. Don't worry, 'Zephaniah' and 'Zechariah' are not answers, so you won't have to worry about keeping those books straight.

1

A NASA spacecraft of this name was launched in 2001 on a mission to gather solar wind. Even though the spacecraft crash-landed, some of the samples it collected were recovered and were used to gain information about the formation of the solar system. What name was also given to two prototype inflatable space modules, launched in 2006 and 2007 for the private space-exploration company Bigelow Aerospace?

2

Francis Bacon said members of this profession should be 'lions under the throne'. Edward

Coke is reported to have told James I that the king did not have 'the artificial reason' required to undertake this profession. What profession is or was practiced by people who have titles such as the Queen's Remembrancer, the Chief Baron of the Exchequer and the Master of the Rolls?

3

One man with this given name delivered the 'Second Reply to Hayne', a speech given at the United States Senate. Another man with this given name wrote the poem 'The True-Born Englishman', as well as several novels. A third man of this name explained the meaning of the cryptic phrase 'mene, mene, tekel, upharsin'. What name means 'God is my judge' in Hebrew?

4

This name appears in the name of the element with the atomic number 104 (named after a physicist) and in the name of the element with the atomic number 44 (named after Russia). This name is also the surname of a man nicknamed 'the Bambino'. What name is also the given name of an Associate Justice of the United States Supreme Court, who is sometimes nicknamed 'the Notorious RBG'?

5

It has been argued that all of these entities are interesting on the basis that an uninteresting one would itself be interesting. A particularly large one of these entities is named after Ronald Graham, while another one of these entities is named after Srinivasa Ramanujan. Types of these entities include: surds, cardinals and transcendentals. What entities can be written using octal, hexadecimal and binary?

6

The Hebrew name for this book translates to 'names', as this book begins with a list of names. This book does not specifically mention Jannes and Jambres, men mentioned in 2 Timothy, but they are identified with unnamed 'sorcerers' mentioned in this book. What book of the Bible includes a description of the construction of the Ark of the Covenant?

7

In a radio address, Senator Huey Long proposed to make every man one of these class of people. Jean-Baptiste Bernadotte, one of Napoleon's Marshals of France, allegedly had a tattoo which called for the death of these people. To which people was Shakespeare referring when he wrote that that some were 'haunted by ghosts', while others were 'poison'd by their wives'?

8

One of the chapters of this book inspired the chorus 'Va, pensiero', sung by the Hebrew slave chorus in Verdi's *Nabucco*. In the King James Version, the word 'selah' frequently appears in this book of the Bible. What book of the Bible includes both its longest chapter and its shortest chapter?

9

This book of the Bible has a name very similar to another book that was included as apocrypha in the King James Version. The name of this book comes from the Greek for 'assembly', as the 'Preacher' mentioned in this book is one who addresses such a group. What book of the Bible includes the line '[H]e who increases knowledge increases sorrow'? (A discouraging sentiment for quizzing fans.)

10

This word is used in the name of the artistic style in which Christ's friends are depicted over his body (Pietà paintings and sculptures are a subgenre of this artistic style that include a depiction of Mary). What word is also used in the name of ancient poems or songs that express regret over the destruction of cities, including examples for Ur, Eridu and Jerusalem?

•

CHAPTER 9: 11 WORDS THAT ARE ASSOCIATED WITH COLOURS

This category should add some colour to the book. Each answer is a word that comes from the name of a colour in a different language.

1

This word for a type of direction comes from the Latin word for 'red ochre', specifically because the Romans used to write directions in red ink, so they stood out on the page. The word can also be used to refer to instructions for church services. The word 'black' is somewhat contradictorily used to describe a particular example of these directions in the Book of Common Prayer. What term is now also used to describe the criteria on which academic tasks are judged?

2

The first syllable in the name of this tea comes from a Chinese word for 'light black'. This tea is not to be mistaken for what in the West is referred to as 'black tea' (which is known by syllables meaning 'red tea' in Chinese). Unlike regular (black) tea, the leaves of this 'light black' tea are only partially oxidised. What is the name of a tea whose second syllable means 'dragon'?

3

This word is used to refer to a political party in Paraguay, the party of former President Alfredo Stroessner. Perhaps surprisingly, the party is not a socialist party (though neither is the United States Republican party, despite its official colour). The word is also used to refer to a state of the United States of America where John Kerry and Karl Rove were born. What word means 'coloured red' in Spanish?

4

The local name of the southern coast of France is linked by this mineral to a place in Central Asia. The southern coast of France has a colour in its name. The same word for the colour is used in several languages, including French and English, and is derived from the name of the mineral. What blue mineral, famously used in the ancient *Ram in a Thicket* sculptures, has a name that in turn comes from the Central Asian location where it was mined? The *Ram in a Thicket* sculptures are famously beautiful and valuable – if 'black sheep' is a derogatory term, perhaps 'blue sheep' should be a term of praise.

5

The words used for this type of animal in several different languages come from circumlocutions, lest using the fearsome animal's 'true' name will attract it. In Russian, the word used for this animal refers to its favourite food. In English and several other languages, the word used for this animal refers to its brown colour. What family of mammals includes carnivorous and herbivorous species, not all of which are brown?

6

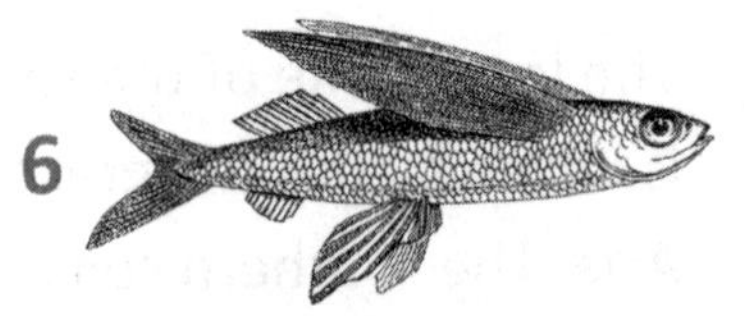

Depending on the other words with which it is combined, this word can refer to a variety of small objects or alternately to a species of large animals. The word distinguishes the small objects in question, as well as certain fish, from *sevruga* and *ossetia* varieties (the small objects are produced by the fish). What word, which comes from the Russian word for 'white', is also used to describe a species of whale?

7

Albinus was a Roman surname. One notable person with this surname was Clodius Albinus, a Governor of Britain who unsuccessfully proclaimed himself Emperor. (Perhaps there was some reason Claudius successfully became Emperor, but Clodius did not.) The word 'albedo' refers to the reflectiveness of a surface. The Latin word for what colour links the name 'Albinus' and the word 'albedo' with the words 'album' and 'albumen'?

8

One name of this ancient people may come from the Greek word for the colour of blood, referring to a product they produced. Unless, that is, the name of the colour came from the name of the people... The name of this ancient people is also associated with a genus of date palms and with a mythical bird. What people, associated with an early alphabet, lived in Tyre and Sidon and, according to tradition, founded Carthage?

9

The original person described as performing this role was François Leclerc du Tremblay, also known as Père Joseph. Père Joseph, a Capuchin friar, is associated with the political machinations of Cardinal Richelieu. The name given to his role may have come from the relative drabness of his habit compared to the red robes of the cardinal. What term is now used to refer to someone who exercises power surreptitiously?

10

The term 'Porphyrogenitus' was used to refer to princes of this empire. The term means 'born to the purple', as empresses of this empire gave birth in a room lined with porphyry, a glittering igneous rock with a name coming from the Greek word for 'purple'. The name commonly used to refer to this empire today was not current before the empire's fall. What empire followed a branch of Christianity in which worshippers venerated icons, except during periods of iconoclasm?
One would imagine the pop star Prince must have been a latter-day son of this empire.

11

This city gives its name to a series of European Union regulations concerning which member states are responsible for handling applications for asylum. The name of this city, when translated into English, is the same as that of a different city in the northwest of England. Which city, whose name translates to 'black pool', was the birthplace of Jonathan Swift?

•

MATHS AND SCIENCE

It's not a Monkman & Seagull Quiz Book *without a category on maths and science.*

CHAPTER 10: 10 MATHS AND SCIENCE

Maths, dull? There are many negative preconceptions about science, nerds and formulae. But actually, it's a fascinating world of huge personalities (living and dead), intellectual duelling and stranger-than-science-fiction discoveries. Like language, maths is everywhere in our lives, from the supermarket to adverts on TV. Don't fear maths and science; see them as a code to unlocking the secrets of the universe.

1

The number pi can be approximated by using this representation of arctangent function, taking the value at 1 and multiplying by four. Certain results that can be obtained by this representation were known to Madhava, a mathematician from a location in what is now India. Others were known to James Gregory in the 17th century. What is the name of the representation of a mathematical function as a (potentially) infinite sum of polynomial function?

2

This phenomenon can become destructive if a smaller celestial body gets within the Roche limit of a larger one. Near black holes, this phenomenon can cause 'spaghettification'. It can also cause the rotation of a body to become synchronised with its revolution around another body. What is the name for this phenomenon, which on Earth comes in 'spring' and 'neap' varieties?

3

Scientists have determined that these objects can change form, thus implying that they have mass. They were hypothesised by Wolfgang Pauli in order to account for a missing particle in a certain form of radioactive decay. What elusive objects are studied at Sudbury, Canada and at the Kamiokande observatory in Hida, Japan?

4

A formula for calculating this quantity is carved on Ludwig Boltzmann's tombstone in Vienna.

The 'Maxwell's demon' thought experiment presents a scenario in which it appears as if this quantity could decrease. The fate that befell Humpty Dumpty is sometimes given as a humourous illustration of one of its governing laws. What physical quantity can roughly be described as the amount of energy in a system that is not available to do work?

5

The application of Pauli's exclusion principle to electrons explains why these celestial objects do not collapse. Subrahmanyan Chandrasekhar determined that the maximum mass of one of these objects is 1.44 solar masses, a limit that now bears his name. If one of these objects absorbs sufficient matter from another body, a Type-1a supernova could result. What object has a sometimes-inaccurate name, as they are not all the same colour?

6

According to physicist Alan Guth, the Universe went through a rapid period of a phenomenon with this name within the first few seconds of its existence. A very different phenomenon of this same name occurred across Western Europe in the 16th century, possibly as a result of a new influx of silver from what is now Mexico and Bolivia. What term is used in physics to refer to the expansion of the universe and in economics to refer to generally rising prices?

7

This form of information storage gets its name from the fact that devices can retrieve information from it equally quickly, regardless of where the information is stored. It follows that the order in which the information is stored is not important, a discovery which broke the hearts of librarians worldwide. Unlike for CD-ROMs, Incan *quipu* knot-records and shelves of books, continuous electric power is required to maintain this form of information storage. What form of information storage has an acronym that is the same as the English word for the first sign of the zodiac?

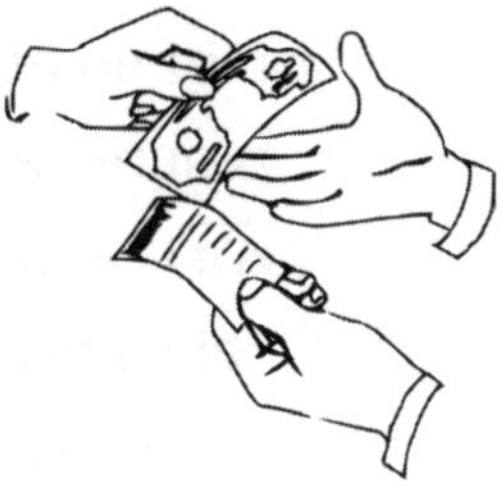

8

The fundamental theorem of algebra requires this type of number to be valid. Counting numbers of this type, the number 1 has three unique cube roots. One of these numbers can be represented as a vector on an Argand diagram (pictured bottom right). What type of number may have both a real component and an imaginary component (for example, 19 + 87i)?

9

The definition of this substance depends in part on its location. Specifically, this substance is outside of something, rather than inside. *A'a* is a rough, sometimes jagged form of this substance, while *pahoehoe* is a ropy, ridged form. *Pele's hair* is a glass form of this substance. This substance can be either in liquid or solid form and can be found at Kilauea in Hawaii. What substance, in its molten state, can cool to form extrusive igneous rocks?

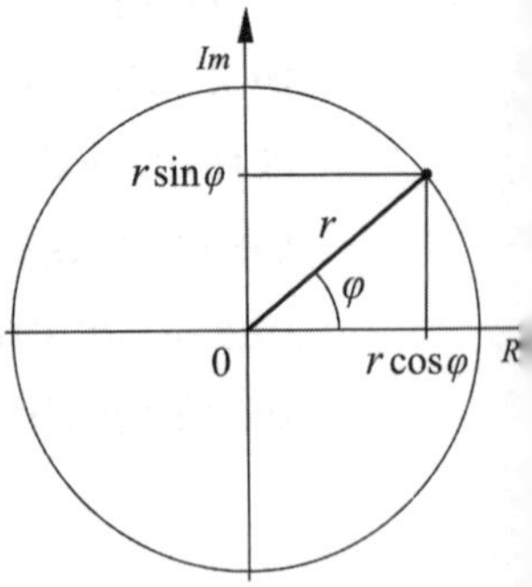

10

Some scientists believe that some individuals of this organism practiced burial customs. Fossils of this organism have been found in a German valley, in Engis, Belgium and in Gibraltar. Indeed, certain marks in stone found in a Gibraltarian cave have led some scientists to believe that some individuals of this organism may have been artistic. What organism has a skull with a prominent brow ridge and a 'bun' on its back?

•

CHAPTER 11:
10 UNITS

Forget pounds-versus-kilograms or quarts-versus-litres. This category deals with some of the odder, less frequently-used units of measurement.

1

Students at MIT measured the Harvard bridge using this unit of length, which was equal to the height of an undergraduate with this name. (The bridge measured 364.4 of these units, plus or minus an ear.) Another individual of this name shared the Nobel Prize in physics for his studies of the cosmic microwave background. What name is also shared by an American Senator from Utah who sponsored a tariff act with Representative Willis Hawley?

2

This unit is (very appropriately) a measure of liquid volume. It is equal to 72 logs, and it appears in the Bible. The unit shares its name with a city in Somerset; the location of the Royal Crescent, The Circus and Pulteney Bridge.

What name also appears in an order of knighthood that was established by George I and has as its motto *'Tria Iuncta In Uno'*?

3

In nuclear physics, this unit has a precise measurement of 10 nanoseconds. In colloquial speech, two of these units can simply mean 'a very short period of time'. The name of the unit can also be used to describe an action. For example, in Haggai 2:7, the LORD Almighty says that he will do this to 'all nations'. What word is also used as a short form for a frothy and delicious blended dairy beverage?

4

This unit appears in the original proverb that is usually translated as 'The journey of a thousand miles begins with a single step.' The unit is sometimes referred to as a 'Chinese mile', though it may originally have denoted a unit of effort (so that one would travel more of these units walking the same distance uphill than downhill). The word for what unit could also be 51 for a Roman?

5

This name can refer to a unit of electric quadrupole (the unit is named after a chemist). It is also used in the name of a 'pi theorem' used in dimensional analysis (the theorem is named after a physicist). The name is also used for a private university in England. What name appears in the name of a residence that once belonged to dukes of this name, but now holds more distinguished occupants?

6

A unit of time equal to six months was jocularly named after a newspaper columnist (he frequently used that length of time when discussing the Iraq War). What unit also shares its name with a musician, humourist and independent candidate for Governor of Texas, as well as with an economist particularly associated with monetarism and the Chicago School?

7

The word for this unit of weight comes from a Latin word for a small pebble. The unit was used by apothecaries, and is equal to around 1.3 grams. With a slightly different meaning, this word was used by Cicero, who used it as an analogy to a matter that vexes the conscience, just as a small stone can vex the body. What word is used to refer to an ethical principle that prevents one from engaging in wrongdoing?

8

The term for these units is sometimes used to refer to quantities of mass and sometimes to quantities of volume. Exactly what the term for these units refers to varies, depending on the substance being measured. For example, one microgram of vitamin D equals 40 of these units, while 1 microgram of retinol (vitamin A) is equal to 3.33 of these units. What units, abbreviated IU, are used to standardise quantities of medically-active substances?

9

This unit denotes a distance, not an amount of time. It is used to describe very long distances. This unit is equal to the distance from the earth an object would need to be to appear to move by one arcsecond if an observer were to move the distance from the earth to sun. Alternate names proposed for this unit include the 'astron' and the 'seriometer'. What unit of length is equal to around 3.26 light years?

10

Units of mass, time, charge, temperature and length are named after this German physicist. One special property of his namesake units is that they are defined based on the values of fundamental constants, rather than on arbitrary, human-derived quantities. What physicist is also famous for his theory that energy comes in fixed amounts called quanta?

•

CHAPTER 12: 10 EQUATIONS AND STATEMENTS

Match these equations and statements with the scientist or mathematician who is usually associated with them (the list of names follows the equations). Don't all rush to the obvious ones.

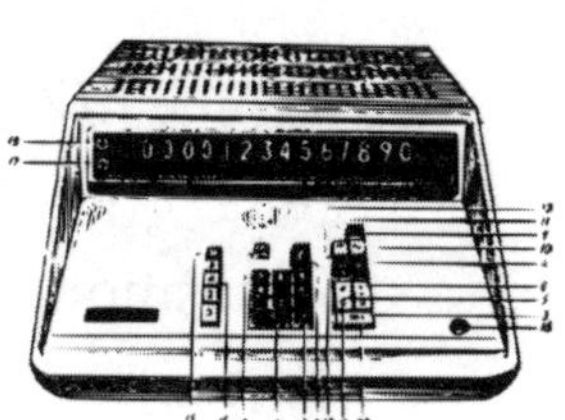

1

$P_1V_1 = P_2V_2$

(P is pressure, V is volume.)

2

P(A|B) = P(B|A)P(A)/P(B)

(P(X) is the probability of observing X, P(X|Y) is the probability of observing X given one has observed Y).

3

F = kx

(F is force, x is distance, k is a constant.)

4

$A^2 = B^2 + C^2$

(B and C are the lengths of the legs of a triangle, A is the length of the hypotenuse)

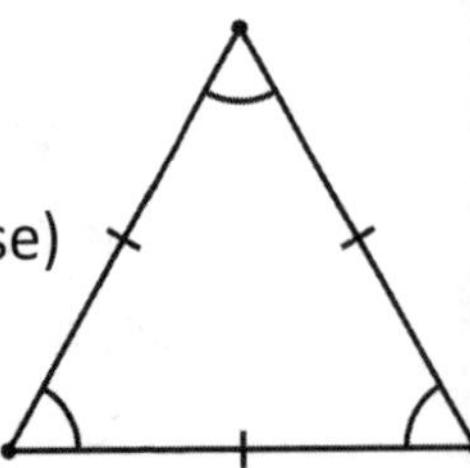

5

$\Delta x \Delta p \geq \hbar/2$

(Δx is uncertainty in position, Δp is uncertainty in position, $\hbar$ is Planck's constant divided by 2π.)

6

$i \approx r + \pi$

(valid for small r and π; i is the nominal interest rate, r is the real interest rate and π the rate of inflation.)

7

$F = GMm/r^2$

(F is force, M the mass of the first object, m the mass of the second object, r the distance between the objects and G a constant.)

8

$e^{i\pi} = -1$

(e is 2.71828...; π is 3.14159...; i is √(-1))

9

$E = mc^2$

(E is energy, m is mass, c is the speed of light.)

10

$A^n \neq B^n + C^n$ where $n > 2$

(A, B, C and n are positive whole numbers.)

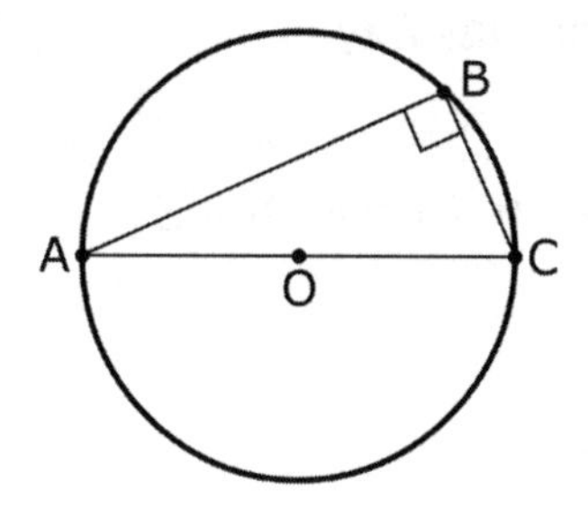

a. Albert Einstein

b. Irving Fisher

c. Robert Boyle

d. Isaac Newton

e. Pythagoras

f. Robert Hooke

g. Pierre de Fermat

h. Leonhard Euler

i. Thomas Bayes

j. Werner Heisenberg

CHAPTER 13: 10 DISCREDITED THEORIES

The accumulation of scientific knowledge is not a smooth progression. Theories that everyone accepts are overturned by new knowledge and ideas. This category looks at some of the ideas that did not make it, and their unfortunate proponents: immortalised for all the wrong reasons.

1

This theory was satirised in Wolfgang Amadeus Mozart's *Cosi Fan Tutte*. According to this theory, living beings are connected by some vital force, which can be manipulated in order to cure disease. Followers of this theory recommended consumption of iron, massage and bringing patients into a trance state. What theory is named after an Austrian physician whose name is now used in a word for hypnotism or for very intense fascination?

2

This man proposed a theory of celestial mechanics in which the sun and the moon orbit the earth, while the other planets orbit the sun. He set up an observatory on the Island of Hven (now known as Ven), and later served as Imperial Mathematician to Rudolf II. He observed a supernova in 1572, providing evidence against the Aristotelian view that the heavens do not change. What Danish astronomer hired Johannes Kepler as an assistant?

3

Some of Rudyard Kipling's tales in the *'Just So' Stories* describe natural changes consistent with this theory. In one form, this theory postulates that the movement of certain fluids within an animal's body can change its physiology. The theory is particularly associated with a French naturalist affiliated with the *Jardin des Plantes* in Paris. What theory posits that organisms change during their lifetimes in response to natural challenges, and that these changes are hereditary?

4

The terms 'choleric', 'phlegmatic', 'melancholy' and 'sanguine' come from the theory of these substances. According to the theory, these substances are present in the body, and the proper balance between these substances is necessary to maintain good health. Galen and Hippocrates are associated with the introduction of the theory of these substances. What was the term used for four different substances in a now-discredited medical theory?

5

A fossil allegedly belonging to this non-existant organism was discovered in East Sussex in 1912. It was given the name *Eoanthropus dawsoni*. Evidence for the existence of this organism included skull fragments, teeth and a simian-like jawbone. This organism was hypothesised to be a 'missing link' between humans and other apes. The fossil remains of what alleged organism were shown in 1953 to be forgeries made of painted human skull fragments and an orangutan jaw?

6

The name for this practice may come from a Greek word for Egypt. Strictly speaking, the practice is not entirely pseudoscientific; Ernest Rutherford partially achieved the ultimate aim. The god Hermes Trismegistus is associated with this practice, and was supposed to have invented a way to make glass airtight. What practice is associated with Isaac Newton, Roger Bacon and John Dee?

7

This pseudoscience is believed to have inspired the theft of Joseph Haydn's skull. Franz Josef Gall was an early pioneer of this pseudoscience, inspired by correlations he noticed between his acquaintances' facial features and their character traits. The psychograph was an instrument used to make measurements relevant to this pseudoscience. What pseudoscience was based around a supposed connection between the shape of the skull and mental abilities?

8

This hypothetical substance needed to be sufficiently solid to allow for the propagation of high-frequency transverse waves through it. On the other hand, it needed to be so vaporous that solid objects could move through it without difficulty. Michelson and Morley conducted an experiment that provided no evidence for the existence of this substance. Einstein's special theory of relativity rendered this substance unnecessary to explain natural phenomena. What substance was hypothesised to exist as a medium for the propagation of light waves?

9

This model of the atom was introduced by physicist JJ Thomson following his identification of the electron. According to this mode, atoms consist of a 'sea' of positive charge in which electrons are embedded. Ernest Rutherford proved that this model does not accurately represent the atom following his 'gold foil' experiment. What model of the electron has a name similar to the name of a Christmas dessert?

10

In one version of this theory of the universe, matter would need to somehow be 'added' to the universe to ensure it maintained a constant density. This theory of the universe allowed for the fact that the universe is expanding. The discovery of the cosmic microwave background was inconsistent with this theory. What theory was created in opposition to the now widely accepted Big Bang theory?

•

CHAPTER 14: 10 NO DIMINISHING RETURNS TO KNOWLEDGE! – BUSINESS, ECONOMICS AND FINANCE

Whether you're topping up your petrol before a long journey, checking when to buy your holiday euros or even planning your purchase of the chocolate bar Freddo (used to be 10p in our childhood – but now much more!), the world of money plays a key role in our daily lives. Both Eric and Bobby have had experience in the corporate world: Eric in finance journalism, and Bobby as a trader in investment banking and as a chartered accountant. In fact, Bobby was a junior trader at the American investment bank Lehman Brothers on that infamous day on Monday 15th September 2008 when Lehman Brothers collapsed (and no, it was not Bobby's fault).

1

Situated about halfway between Birmingham and London, what large town in the UK was formally designated a New Town on 23rd January 1967? The first word in this town's name is the first name of the winner of the 1976 Nobel Prize for Economics, who was an advisor to both President Reagan and Prime Minister Thatcher. The second word is the surname of the author of the seminal work of 1936, *The General Theory of Employment, Interest and Money*.

2

Not to be confused with a playful form of flirtation carried out through podic contact, the FTSE 100 (pronounced 'Footsie One Hundred') is a barometer for the general financial health of companies, regulated by UK company law. The FTSE 100 is a collection of the 100 largest companies by market capitalisation listed on the UK financial markets. What do the initials FTSE stand for?

3

What surname links the following people: the rich corporate banker played by Richard Gere in the 1990 film *Pretty Woman* (Bobby confesses to having first seen this only recently); the financial journalist author of top-selling books that became Hollywood films (*Moneyball* and *The Big Short*) and the British man who created the website MoneySavingExpert.com?

4

When drinking a nice cup of Tetley tea, driving your Jaguar or Land Rover, or sitting in your office under a Volta air conditioner (the leading market brand) you are using products belonging to which large Indian conglomerate founded in Mumbai in 1868? The four-letter name also means 'goodbye', especially in the North-West of England but also used by Tigger in the 1988-91 *The New Adventures of Winnie the Pooh* cartoons.

5

Yugoslavia in 1994, Hungary in 1946, Greece in 1944, Zimbabwe in 2008 and the Weimar Republic in Germany in 1923 experienced the peak period of experiencing what economic phenomenon? This term is an extreme case of monetary inflation so fast and out of control that regular concepts of value and price are rendered meaningless.

6

Kenneth Grahame, the Scottish author of *The Wind in the Willows,* was a senior employee at which institution for 30 years? In 1903, he avoided being shot by a man dubbed a 'Socialist Lunatic' who entered his place of work. A year afterwards, Grahame began writing his classic children's novel, and resigned four months before the publication of the book, in 1908. The assailant shot three times but we must praise the literature gods that each bullet missed, otherwise we may have missed out on the inimitable characters of Mole, Ratty and Mr Toad.

7

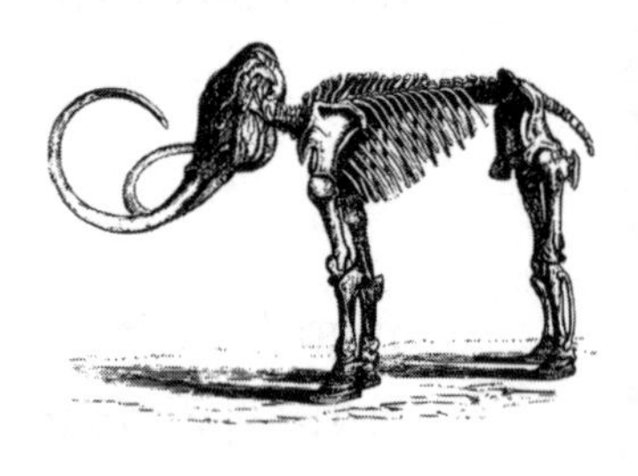

'No, Mr Bond, I expect you to die.' These were the words of James Bond's evil nemesis in the 1964 film *Goldfinger*. Mr Bond had uncovered Auric Goldfinger's plan to contaminate the United States Bullion Depository at Fort Knox. Holding roughly 2-5% of all the gold ever refined in human history, what American state is Fort Knox situated in? Named for a word meaning 'meadowland', this state is where 'Mammoth Cave', the largest known cave system in the world, is located, and is also where the tune for 'Happy Birthday To You' originates.

8

Ancient Carthage (in modern-day Tunisia) is said to have been the first place to have issued lightweight bank notes. However the first known bank note was developed during the era of which Chinese dynasty? Merchants wanted to avoid the heavy bulk of carrying copper coinage in large commercial transactions. This period is sometimes referred to as the Golden Age of Ancient China, and also includes the invention of woodblock printing and gunpowder.

9

Before it existed officially as an entity, what engine was originally nicknamed 'Backrub' by its founders, in a research project for their dissertation? Eventually the name was changed: to a misspelling of a number that is the digit 1 followed by one hundred zeroes (trust an expert Maths teacher: this is a very, very big number). While the company's motto is still 'Don't be evil', following a corporate restructuring, the new parent company called 'Alphabet Inc.' has the motto 'Do the right thing'.

10

A sherry and beaten egg for William Gladstone, a brandy and water for both Benjamin Disraeli and John Major, a spritzer for Nigel Lawson, a gin and tonic for Geoffrey Howe and a whisky for Kenneth Clarke. What is the connection between these choice of beverages and a day that has been described by former Prime Minister Harold Macmillan to be 'rather like a school Speech Day: a bit of a bore, but there it is'.

•

HISTORY

It is said that we cannot understand the present without understanding the past. So let's take a look back at the murky origins of our favourite holidays, learn tolerance by seeing how similar we are to those in far-flung places long ago, and gain a better knowledge of our politicians by comparing them to heroes of the past.

CHAPTER 15: 4 PARALLEL LIVES

Ever since Plutarch's Lives Of The Noble Greeks And Romans, *commonly known as* Parallel Lives, *people have looked for common threads in the lives of famous people; similar virtues or failings. The following questions each have two answers – two different, but similar, people.*

1

Park Chung-Hee and Chiang Ching-kuo both studied abroad, temporarily adopting foreign names. Park gained power through a military coup, while Chiang took the more traditional route and succeeded his father as leader of his country. In office, both men wielded dictatorial powers, and both pursued economic policies that encouraged industrial development by favouring exports. Which countries did the two men respectively serve as presidents?

2

Both of these men came from outside their nations' traditional elites and had humble beginnings to their military careers. One began as a second lieutenant, the other as an *ashigaru* footsoldier. Both would rise to supreme command of their nations based on their military and political genius, though neither would adopt the traditional ruling title: 'king' or 'shogun'. Both engaged in initially successful but ultimately failed foreign campaigns, against Russia and Korea respectively. Who are these two men?

3

Both of these men were endearingly referred to as 'father' by grateful compatriots. Both worked as lawyers and studied law at the University of London (though one did so by distance education). Both worked for political change in their respective countries and spent time in prison as a result of their activities. Both also worked for reconciliation following the partial success of their aims. Who are these two men, one Indian and one South African?

4

Both of these women took up arms against imperial powers that tried to annex their homelands, when said powers challenged the validity of the succession from their royal husbands to their children. Their actions were ultimately unsuccessful, but authors from their erstwhile adversaries would later praise them – I'm sure they'd be very grateful to know it. Name these two women, one who led Britons against the Roman empire, the other who led Indians against the British Raj.

CHAPTER 16: 10 THE ROAD TO D-DAY

The D-Day landings constituted one of the largest amphibious invasions in history. (N.B.: 'amphibious warfare' has nothing to do with frogs, as 'guerrilla warfare' has nothing to do with silverback apes.) A lot of planning and preparation went in to making them a success. This category looks at the events that occurred in the lead-up to the crossings.

1

Various reasons have been given for this military operation. Some claim it was an attempt to distract the German military and take pressure off the Soviet Union. One historian has claimed that it was an attempt to capture a German encryption device. The majority of troops involved in this operation were Canadian. What Allied military failure is sometimes described as a learning experience that contributed to later success at D-Day?

2

The rough date for the D-Day invasions was decided at a Washington DC conference with this codename, attended by Winston Churchill and Franklin Delano Roosevelt. The conference shared this name with a weapon that was wielded by an Ancient Roman 'retiarius' gladiator. In Greek mythology, the weapon in question was used by a god to strike the Athenian Acropolis to open a well of seawater. What name is shared by the conference and the weapon?

3

Propellers, flails, and flamethrowers were added to these large objects in preparation for the D-Day invasion. During the invasion, these objects were used to clear mines from the path of invading soldiers and destroy bunkers and walls. More conventional examples of these objects were used by the German defenders. What objects were known as 'Hobart's funnies', for the modified Allied models, and *panzers* for German models?

4

The Allies tried to convince the Germans that they would attack near this French city, rather than Normandy: General Patton was sent to Dover, across from this place, equipped with rubber tanks and false landing craft. What French city was once a staple port for English products and even belonged to the English Crown until 1558?

5

To spread disinformation in the lead up to D-Day, the Allies also relied on double agents recruited under a system of this name. The system was overseen by what was known as the 'Twenty Committee', a reference to the system's name. What term appears in the name of the system and is more generally used to refer to a situation in which someone ostensibly working for party A against party B is in fact working for party B?

6

To successfully complete an invasion of Europe, the Allies realised they would need to construct artificial harbours. The harbours had a codename that was the name of a type of tree. The trees in question belong to the genus *morus*, and one variety was used to make paper in Imperial China. What tree is particularly associated with the silk industry?

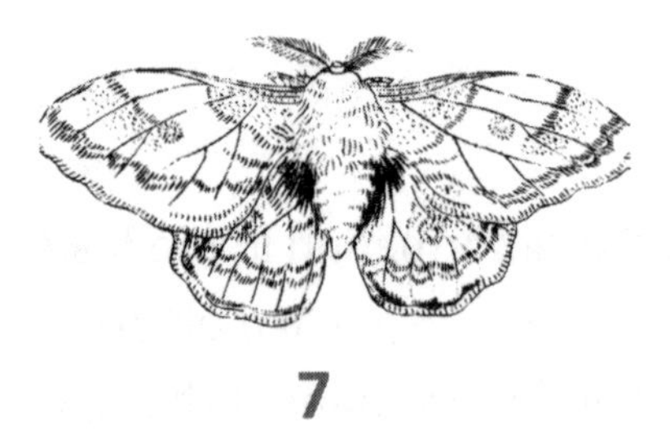

7

First Quote: 'The troops, the air and the Navy did all that bravery and devotion to duty could do. If any blame or fault attaches to the attempt it is mine alone.'
Second Quote: 'The hopes and prayers of liberty-loving people everywhere march with you... I have full confidence in your courage, devotion to duty, and skill in battle. We will accept nothing less than full victory.'
The first quote comes from a message written

before the D-Day invasion in case of failure. (Fortunately, it was never used.) The second quote comes from the Order of the Day issued to troops before the invasion. Who is responsible for both quotations?

8

In anticipation of an attack on the north of France, the Germans transferred this Field Marshal to that area to inspect the defences. He ended up gaining the command of an Army Group assigned to defend Normandy. Unfortunately for him, his wife's birthday was on June 6, and he was back in Germany celebrating with her when the invasion began... Which Field Marshal was nicknamed 'The Desert Fox', and is also famous for commanding German forces in North Africa?

9

Winston Churchill wished to personally watch the D-Day invasion from a British warship. Who is credited as the only man who could convince Churchill to abandon this idea, with the argument that since he himself could not go, it did not seem right that Churchill should be allowed?

10

The 'D-Day Dodgers' was a nickname given to soldiers who avoided D-Day because they were serving here instead. Churchill called this country the 'soft underbelly' of Europe, and thus thought it was a better place to invade than the north of France. What country's mainland was invaded by Allied forces on September 3, 1943?

•

CHAPTER 17:
10 NATIONAL DAYS

Everyone loves a holiday (well, maybe not some employers). This category looks at national holidays around the world and why they are celebrated.

1

The national day of this country occurs on the anniversary of the first day of the Battle of the Somme. For this reason, the national day is also a day of remembrance for a particular region of the country, whose soldiers were hit particularly hard during the battle. The national day of this country used to be called Dominion Day. What country commemorates its confederation on July 1?

2

The national day of this country is determined by an astronomical event, rather than commemorating an historic anniversary. This day is considered a tradition of this country's home rule,

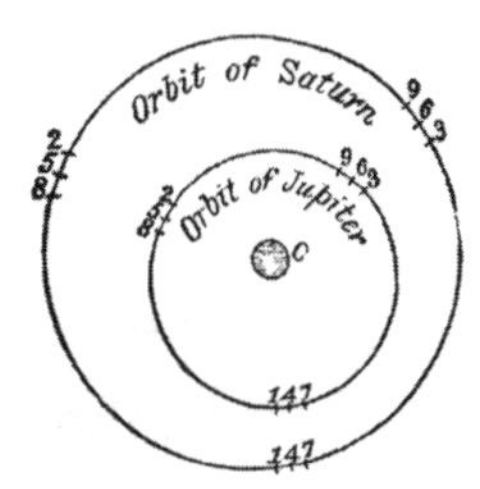

one factor that makes this country distinct from the sovereign state of which it is a part. In some parts of this country, national 'day' is an exactly appropriate term, because the sun does not go below the horizon for the entire 24 hour period of celebration. What country celebrates its national day on the summer solstice?

3

This country celebrates five national holidays. Three of these holidays commemorate the process by which this country became independent from the United Kingdom and a republic, including a day commemorating the withdrawal of British troops from this country. One of these holidays commemorates the death of four rioters in this country at the hands of British troops. What country's fifth national holiday commemorates the victory of the Knights of Saint John over the Ottoman Turks in a siege?

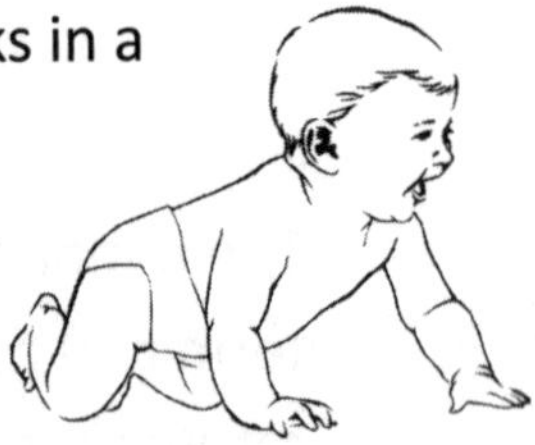

4

The national day of this country is celebrated on the anniversary of the death of a poet from this country. The rather grisly choice of the poet's date of death was chosen for this national day because the date of his birth was unknown (it is believed to have taken place in 1524 or 1525). What country's national day is held on June 10, the day in 1580 when Luis de Camoes, author of the *Lusiads*, died?

5

This territory observes a holiday commemorating an event that took place in 1982. One way in which this holiday is observed is by the placing of wreathes at the Liberation Monument by local notables (including the Governor) and by members of the armed forces. What territory has a holiday on June 14, the anniversary of the last day of a war?

6

The national day of this country commemorates the anniversary of the election of a king and of the adoption of a constitution on the same date 286 years later. In 2005, the day replaced

Whit Monday as a public day off, which led people of this country to complain when this day fell on a weekend. The national day of this country is commemorated by a ceremony at Skansen at which children give flowers to the country's monarchs. Which country celebrates its national day on June 6?

7

This country's national day commemorates an event that took place in 1788, over one hundred years before the country's federation. One way in which this day is celebrated is through the presentation of an annual award to a distinguished citizen of this country. What country's national day takes place on January 26, the anniversary of the arrival of the First Fleet?

8

This country's national day celebrates its independence from the Roman Empire. It is held on the feast day of the saint for whom this country is named and is marked by a procession of the saint's relics. The day also features a crossbow tournament. What small state celebrates Republic Day on September 3?

9

In this country, the national day is simply called 'The National Celebration' in the local language. This day is celebrated in the country's possessions in the Americas and in the South Pacific, as well as in what is referred to as 'The Hexagon'. It is commemorated by a military parade on July 14. What country commemorates what foreigners refer to by the name of a prison?

10

This country's national day commemorates an event that took place in a location now no longer under the *de facto* control of the country. At the time of the event and after, while the country was under martial law, the day was marked with substantial military displays. Military participation in the festivities continues following democratic reforms in this country, but other aspects of the country are now celebrated as well. What country observes a holiday known as 'Double Ten Day' because it takes place on October 10?

•

CHAPTER 18: 10 BEFORE 1000 BC

Eric is particularly fascinated by the world before 1000 BC. Ancient philosophies such as Christianity, Judaism, Buddhism, Confucianism and various ones from Greece connect us internationally now, and bring us closer to people who lived and died 2,000 to 2,500 years ago. However, the intellectual world before the development of these lodestars was completely different from the one we live and think in today. This category is devoted to what was going on at that time, when the act of writing was relatively new.

1

Shutruk-Nahunte, King of Elam, once owned an inscription of this document. Some of this document deals with witchcraft, other parts with the maintenance of dams. One inscription of this document was written on a basalt column that somewhat resembles a gigantic human finger. A carving on the column depicts the god

Shamash, who allegedly composed this document. What ancient document sets out the principle of an 'eye for an eye' for some offences?

2

A tablet from the old Babylonian empire (circa 1800 BC) indicates that the Babylonians were able to solve at least some of these equations by completing the square, so they'd have been able to understand some middle-school Maths lessons, though passing a UK GCSE might have been tough. At present, it is possible to solve these equations by use of a formula. Graphing one of these equations yields a parabola. Along with simple equations, what type of equation did Gilbert and Sullivan's Modern Major General understand?

3

The name of one of the settlements of this Bronze Age civilisation may come from the Sindhi for 'Mound of the Dead'. The inhabitants' own name for the settlement is unknown, as texts left by the people of this civilisation have yet to be

deciphered. (Even today, many people find the iPhone predictive function impossible to use.) There is evidence that this civilisation enjoyed sanitation systems in the third millennium BC, but little evidence it engaged in warfare. What is the name of this civilisation, named after a river that today runs through Pakistan and India?

4

A gold funeral mask discovered by Heinrich Schliemann has been said to belong to this mythical figure. However, the mask has been dated to around 1550-1500 BC, so it was made too early for when this figure may have lived. One daughter of this man was the namesake of a tragedy by Sophocles, while another of his daughters was the namesake of an opera by Gluck. What King of Mycenae was the brother of Menelaus and the husband and victim of Clytemnestra?

5

Remedies for this disease may be described in the Ebers Papyrus, an Egyptian text dated to the 16th century BC. One form of this disease is a result of the destruction or malfunctioning of beta cells in the pancreas. Another form occurs because beta cells do not produce enough insulin and other cells in the body are insulin resistant. What disease also has a 'gestational' form, which affects women during pregnancy?

6

This settlement has been inhabited by many different cultures over a period spanning more than 10,000 years. The site achieved particular prominence as a Canaanite settlement during the Bronze Age. Numerous structures in the settlement have been built and rebuilt many times over the centuries, including the walls. The fall of the walls of what settlement is described in the Book of Joshua, Chapter 6, and in a cheerily destructive gospel song?

7

The taotie pattern appears on bronzeware produced during the reign of this dynasty. This dynasty also saw the production of 'oracle bones': examples of early Chinese writing

carved on ox bones or turtle shells. This dynasty allegedly overthrew the Xia Dynasty, and was eventually toppled by the Zhou. Which Chinese dynasty, which flourished during the 2nd millennium BC, had a capital near the modern city of Anyang?

8

Enheduanna, daughter of King Sargon of Akkad, wrote poetry in the 23rd century BC dedicated to this goddess. One of the gates to the city of Babylon, now reconstructed in the Pergamon Museum in Berlin, was dedicated to her. In the *Epic of Gilgamesh*, she proposes marriage to Gilgamesh, who refuses her at great cost to himself. What Mesopotamian goddess of love and fertility had different names in Akkadian and Sumerian?

9

Groups of people with this belligerent-sounding name are often mentioned in the Pentateuch, alongside the Amorites and the Jebusites (in Deuteronomy 20:17, for example). It is not clear whether the people so mentioned are related to another people who bear the same name. (Though said people's name is about as common as 'Jebusite'.) The latter group who bear this name created an empire that collapsed during the Bronze Age crisis. What name is applied to an ancient Anatolian people, speakers of an Indo-European language?

10

Letters to this man from the kings of Babylon and Assyria have been found in the ruined city of Amarna. The letters are written in cuneiform on clay tablets, not in the famously beautiful script of this man's native land. After this man's death, efforts were taken to eliminate his name from records and to deface his depiction in art. What man was Pharaoh of Egypt in the 14th century BC, and is noted for changing Egypt's religion, and his own name, to honour a sun god?

MISCELLANEOUS KNOWLEDGE

A section on culture both 'pop' and 'high-brow' – though the distinction is arguably less distinguishable nowadays. Don't be fooled into thinking this section will be any easier: there are conundrums ahead.

CHAPTER 19: 20 THE PRICE OF A PINT OF MILK – POP CULTURE

'Are you switched on to everyday things? You might know the astrophysical answer to what happened in 1734 on the moon at 4.30am in the morning, but how much is a pint of milk?''

This is the question asked on national TV by presenter Jeremy Kyle to both Bobby and Eric. Just to reassure readers, this was not a Jeremy Kyle Show *'who's the father?', but was on ITV's* Good Morning Britain, *as part of the promotion of BBC Radio Four's* Monkman & Seagull's Polymathic Adventure. *(Monkman and Seagull will take any opportunity to promote this excellent, informative and humorous programme, which features Stephen Fry among other guests.)*

The question posed by Jeremy-not-Paxman-but-Kyle was trying to play on the fact that classically knowledgeable people (those who might be fans of University Challenge*) might be shielded from the everyday knowledge that you would expect normal people to have from practical life – such as the price of a pint of milk, or the Number One music hit, or the price of a newspaper. And if you are a* *frequent viewer of both Jeremies, your intellectual capacities are remarkable... This is the field of popular culture. Bobby was particularly 'gassed' (that's colloquial slang for 'excited') when, on the ITV studio set, he met Marcel from the smash-hit TV series* Love Island *– his guilty viewing pleasure of summer 2017.* Love Island*, as you know, is a reality dating show that fits comfortably into the genre of 'popular culture'.*

**PS – The answer to Jeremy's question about what happened in 1734 on the moon at 4.30am is 'not much'.*

***PPS – Bobby answered that he buys four pints at a time and hence the answer for major supermarkets is £1.*

Watch this interview on ITV's Good Morning Britain *of Bobby & Eric: https://youtu.be/Pol-1L_sXEo*

1

The British-American rock band Fleetwood Mac released a song called 'The Chain' on their bestselling album of 1978, *Rumours.* (Bobby became a fan of this band after watching an episode of the musical drama *Glee* about Fleetwood Mac.) The instrumental section of the song gained widespread fame in the UK for being the theme tune for the TV coverage of which sport?

2

A mobile gaming craze swept across the globe in 2016 and caused headaches for teachers such as Mr Seagull, with students sneaking from his classroom in search of nearby Caterpie, Charizard or Charmeleon. What free-to-play, location-based, augmented reality game was developed by Niantic and Nintendo in which players attempted to locate fictional monsters?

3

'Shaken, not stirred' is a catchphrase of Ian Fleming's UK secret service agent 007 (aka James Bond). This adjectival phrase described Mr Bond's preference for the preparation of his martini cocktails. The martini is a cocktail made with gin and garnished with an olive or a lemon twist. What other fortified wine is essential for a martini?

4

With its exterior shots of the majestic Highclere Castle in Hampshire, what British historical period drama was created by Julian Fellowes and depicted the lives of the aristocratic Crawley family and their domestic servants in the post-Edwardian era? Dan Stevens, who played Matthew Crawley, is an alumnus of Emmanuel College. American rapper and super-fan Sean Combs (Puff Daddy) was 'not happy about' the ending of which series in 2015?

5

Initially a series of animated shorts, this dysfunctional family of five became a part of *The Tracey Ullman Show* in 1987 and their own show is still going strong in 2017. Leonard Nimoy, Stephen Hawking, Paul & Linda McCartney, U2, Tom Jones and Elizabeth Taylor are among the celebrity names that have appeared in which US animated sitcom?

6

Ravi Shankar, world famous Indian musician, was one of the best-known players of the sitar, a plucked, stringed instrument used in Indian classical music. What is the name of his daughter, an American jazz singer-songwriter who sold more than 50 million records with her albums including *Come Away with Me* and *Feels Like Home*?

7

The crime fiction novels *The Cuckoo's Calling* (2013), *The Silkworm* (2014), and *Career of Evil* (2015) have all been published under the pseudonym Robert Galbraith. Although the author's true identity was unexpectedly unveiled in a twist worthy of a crime novel itself, what is the real name of the author? They continue to use this pseudonym to maintain distinction from their other writings.

8

Born in Ghana but moving to London when still a child, this man's life took a U-turn at the age of 16 when he was spotted on a train by stylist

Simon Foxton. After a brief career in modelling, he became the youngest-ever fashion director for an international publication. Following in the footsteps of Alexandra Shulman, who became the first male editor-in-chief of fashion magazine *British Vogue* in 2017?

9

Napoleon Bonaparte, Billy the Kid, Socrates, Sigmund Freud, Genghis Khan, Abraham Lincoln and Ludwig van Beethoven all starred as characters in which 1989 science-fiction comedy, starring a young Keanu Reeves? Two friends travel through time to gather together a collection of historical figures for their high school history presentation. (Monkman & Seagull also travel through time together, normally one second into the future per second.)

10

Based on an original Japanese series translated as 'Tigers of Money', the British TV show *Dragons' Den* allows entrepreneurs to pitch their business ideas to wealthy investors. Ideas have ranged from the fabulous Levi Roots' fabulous table sauces to hare-brained schemes such as the pet burial pack and cardboard furniture. What is the name of the US equivalent of the same franchise? It shares its first name with a group of elasmobranch fish.

11

The family known as The Firm quietly changed their name in 1917 because of anti-German feeling during the First World War. What was the previous royal surname?

12

Trey Parker and Matt Stone created the American adult animated sitcom *South Park*, which Bobby might just be a little bit of a fan of in the spare moments between *Downton, Love Island, The Simpsons* and *Glee*. After watching the *Sesame Street*-inspired *Avenue Q* musical conceived by Robert Lopez, they went on to collaborate with Robert to create which 2011 musical comedy about two missionaries who travel to Africa?

13

Instagram launched a standalone app in 2015 that allows users to stitch together photographs to create gif-like videos (Fun fact: 'gif' stands for Graphics Interchange Format). Sharing its name with an indigenous Australian hunting weapon, what is the name of this app? In both digital and non-digital forms, it is a most useful instrument at graduation day hat-throwing.

14

Although first invented as early as 1993, this toy became popular again in 2017. What is this stress-relieving toy, advertised as a help to those who have trouble focusing, but banned in several British schools? They certainly don't help the teachers focus.

15

Despite the UK giving *'nul points'* to ABBA's Eurovision winner 'Waterloo' in 1974, the British public have always been fond of this unusual contest with its hodgepodge collection of Euro-

pean pop acts – from the Russian grannies to an Irish turkey. Yes. A singing, Irish turkey. As entrants, Azerbaijan and Israel stretch the definition of 'Euro', but what is the farthest-flung country to be part of this competition?

16

Comedian Alistair McGowan, politician Diane Abbott, documentary maker Louis Theroux, scientist Dame Mary Archer, journalist John Simpson and foodie Loyd Grossman. They have all appeared in which UK television show?

17

English astronomer Fred Hoyle first came up with a term during a BBC radio broadcast in 1949. It was perhaps intended to be dismissive, but has since become commonplace, and was used as part of the title of which American TV sitcom? Every episode is titled in the format of a scientific theory, excluding the pilot, which is called 'Pilot'.

Despite the show's characters oozing with brains, only one actor (Mayim Bialik, who plays Amy) actually has a real-life PhD.

18

With twin blue plaques outside the wall commemorating these extraordinary flatmates,

what two musicians, separated by two centuries, lived in 23 and 25 Brook Street in Mayfair, London? Once separate buildings but now interconnected, one of the pair wrote *The Messiah* there in 1741, and the other, perhaps the greatest rock guitarist of all time, called the house 'my first real home'.

19

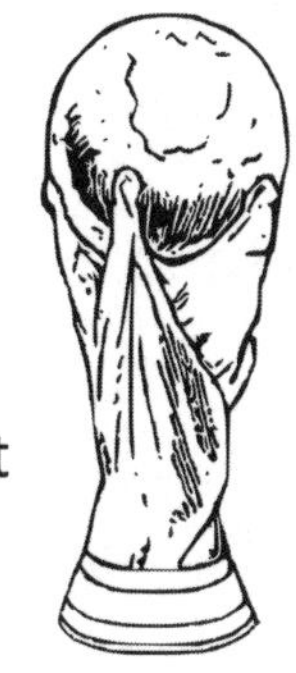

What two initials are shared by the top-level Internet domain for Equatorial Guinea and an international monthly men's magazine based in New York City? Grime artist Stormzy was handed the best solo artist prize by Labour leader Jeremy

Corbyn at this magazine's UK 2017 'Men of the Year' awards. Our very own quiz author Bobby Seagull was interviewed by this magazine's Facebook Live feature back in April 2017.

20

Jereboam, Rehoboam, Methuselah, Salmanzar, Belshazzar, Nebuchadnezzar are names that come from historical figures, predominantly from the Bible. These are also names referring to the size of which type of vessel?

•

CHAPTER 20: 10 'BEST PICTURE' WINNERS OF THE PAST 10 YEARS (2006 TO 2016)

The answers to the questions in this category are all also (roughly) the names of winners of a famous award for Best Picture over the years from 2006 to 2016.

1

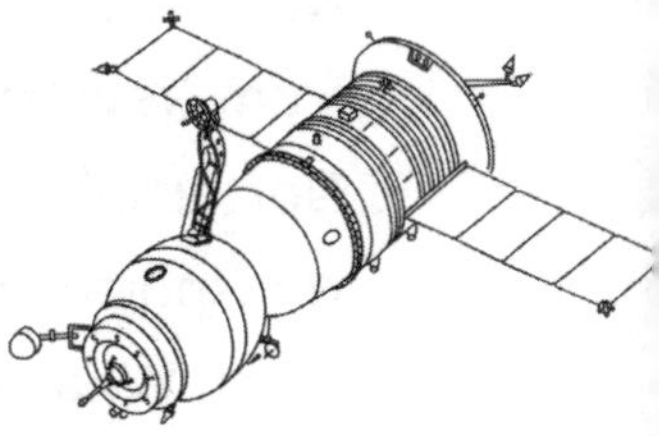

The name of a famous piece of music by Claude Debussy can be translated into a word for this radiation. Beethoven's *Piano Sonata No. 14 in C# Minor 'Quasi una fantasia'* is also often nicknamed for this radiation. What is the name for solar radiation that is reflected from a satellite of Earth?

2

A predecessor of this device operated by heating calcium oxide, also known as quicklime. Currently, these devices use electricity to create light. The title of ABBA's 1980 single 'Super

Trouper' refers to a specific brand of this kind of device. What is the name of a device that creates a beam of light that is used to follow an actor around a stage?

3

This memoir was written by Solomon Northrup, an African-American gentleman from New York State. The memoir describes Northrup's life experience of being kidnapped, transported to New Orleans and sold as a slave. What is the name of this slave narrative, the inspiration for a film of the same name?

4

This vessel was named after a shipwright, not after a 100-eyed giant. The goddess Athena may have assisted in its construction. It was able to successfully sail between Scylla and Charybdis with the help of the nereids. Orpheus, Hercules, Castor and Pollux all sailed on this vessel. What is the name of this legendary ship? The vessel also gives its name to a constellation which is subdivided into the smaller constellations Puppis, Vela and Carina.

5

Henry Wadsworth Longfellow wrote 'Dead he is not, but departed, for [someone in this line of work] never dies.' However, more cynically, PR director Elizabeth Shaw did draw a line between dead and living, noting that dead people of this profession 'always bring out an older, richer crowd.' Shakespeare adds that 'In framing [someone of this profession], Art has thus decreed, / To make some good, but others to exceed.' What would a person of this profession be known as?

6

'I go from a corruptible to an incorruptible Crown, where no disturbance can be, no disturbance in the World' are words from an historical example of one of these. An exhortation by a commander to his 'band of brothers' in a Shakespeare play is a fictional example of one of these. Likewise, state openings of the British Parliament included what form of address, at least before 1952?

7

The title of this film comes from slang for an unpleasant place into which one does not wish to go. No, it's not *The Office: The Movie*. The story for the film was written by a journalist who had been embedded with soldiers during the Iraq War. What is the name of this film, which details the experiences of an Explosive Ordnance Disposal (EOD) unit?

8

This film is based on a book originally titled *Q & A*, a less-than-ultimate title for a book about a quiz. One potential actor for this film turned down the opportunity to play a character representing himself at work, because he did not want people to think

he would actually act like the character in his professional situation. 'Benjamin Franklin', 'Cambridge Circus' and 'Aramis' are correct answers given in this film. What film, directed by Danny Boyle and scored by AR Rahman, is framed around a game show?

9

The title of this film comes from a poem by William Butler Yeats. The film was described as crossing over five different genres by *The Guardian*. What 2007 Coen Brothers film was based on a novel by Cormac McCarthy?

10

This film was a remake of the Hong Kong film *Infernal Affairs*. Instead of triads, the film involves the Irish mob in Boston. The plot involves a double infiltration (the police place a mole in the mob, while the mob place a mole in the police). What is this film, directed by Martin Scorsese?

•

CHAPTER 21: 10 NON-CAPITAL CITIES

The answers to the following questions all involve important cities that are neither capital cities nor the most populous cities in their respective countries, but distinguish themselves in a less obvious manner.

1

A battle between the forces of the United Nations and North Korean soldiers took place around the 'Perimeter' of this city. Access to this port city helped the United Nations forces win the battle, as they were able to import manpower and material. What city is now the second-largest city in South Korea? (Careful with your B's and P's; though either is an acceptable answer.)

2

Perhaps this place cannot really be considered a 'Second City'. While there are indeed fewer *Cariocas* than *Paulistas*, the city in question was the national capital until 1960. It also con-

tains several landmarks considered iconic of its country, including Copacabana Beach and a statue of Christ the Redeemer. What is the name of this Brazilian city, the host of the 2014 FIFA World Cup Final and the 2016 Summer Olympic Games?

3

Sir Norman Haworth and Sir Edmund Hirst first synthesized this substance in 1934 in Birmingham, England. Humans need this substance to produce collagen (and for other purposes). Unlike some animals, humans cannot naturally produce it. What is this substance, which British sailors famously obtained by consuming juice from citrus fruits?

4

The Jagiellonian University is located in this city. One famous graduate of the Jagiellonian was Karol Wojtyła, who later served as Archbishop of this place and still later became Pope John Paul II (the university has great graduate career prospects). Which ancient city contains the fortress Wawel, historically a residence of the kings of Poland?

5

This city began as a settlement of Ionian Greeks from Phocaea. A notable early resident was Pytheas, an explorer. Much later, the city would give its name to an emblematic and violent song that was actually written in Strasbourg. What large city is the capital of the Provence-Alpes-Côte d'Azur region and is located on the Mediterranean coast of France?

6

Between 1757 and 1842, trade between China and European countries was conducted by 'hong merchants' located in this city. More recently, there have been proposals that this city merge with Foshan, Dongguan, Huizhou, Zhaoqing, Jiangmen, Zhongshan, Shenzhen and Zhuhai to form a megacity. What city is the third-largest city in China and the largest in the Pearl River Delta?

7

The Montreal Protocol, signed in 1989, is an agreement to reduce the use of certain compounds that deplete this substance. For example, chlorofluorocarbons release chlorine in the upper atmosphere, which in turn catalyzes the transformation of this substance into oxygen gas. (You could call it a celestial substance: it's heavenly and could be called holy.) What substance has a name that comes from the Greek word 'to smell'?

8

Like Raymond Chandler's *The Big Sleep*, which partly inspired it, this film takes place in Los Angeles. Its soundtrack includes the pieces 'Hotel California' (in Spanish), 'Just Dropped In (To See What Condition My Condition Was In)' and Mozart's *Requiem Mass*. What film involves a Busby Berkeley-inspired dream sequence centred around bowling?

9

Sports teams associated with this city include the Victory Football Club, the Vixens and the Western Bulldogs. Test cricket and Australian Rules Football were pioneered in the city. What city served as the capital of Australia until 1927?

10

By tradition, people from this former Hanseatic port city (especially current and former senators) are not supposed to accept honours in the form of orders. Helmut Schmidt, a former senator from this city, followed this rule. According to John Lennon, The Beatles found 'new ways of playing' as a result of long gigs in this city. What city on the Elbe was the birthplace, perhaps of a certain fast food, and certainly of Johannes Brahms?

CHAPTER 22: 20 AMAZING WOMEN

Both Monkman and Seagull have learned from many amazing women: mothers, grandmothers, sisters, cousins and, outside of the home, friends and teachers. This next section is about distinctive individual women who have influenced the wider world around them.

1

This American writer and civil-rights activist shot to international acclaim following the publication of a book describing the difficulty of finding a voice. It was published in the year of the first moon landing (yes, let's not reiterate conspiracies: the moon landing did happen). Having recited her poem 'On the pulse of the morning' at the inauguration of President Bill Clinton, it is her first autobiography *I Know Why The Caged Bird Sings* that still claims public plaudits after her death in 2014.

2

Spinning faster than Michael Jackson in his prime, pulsars are rotating neutron stars that are often about the size of a city but the mass of our sun. (Something's clearly been raiding the astronomical fridge for midnight snacks!) As a PhD student at Cambridge, what Irish astrophysicist discovered radio pulsars? Unfairly, this Dame did not receive the Nobel Prize in Physics for the discovery, as did her supervisor Anthony Hewish and co-recipient astronomer Martin Ryle, who worked on the same project.

3

Born during the First World War in 1916, this woman's husband, Solomon, was prime minister of her country. After the assassination of her husband by a Buddhist monk, she transformed herself from a quiet housewife to a charismatic political figure, causing her party to choose her as leader in 1960. Who was this woman, the modern world's first female head of government, who served as Prime Minister of Sri Lanka three times?

4

Sometimes known as the 'The First Lady of Football' (soccer, for our North American friends), having been appointed as Managing Director of Birmingham City football club at the tender age of 23, what baroness became the youngest managing director of a UK PLC? Appearing as an aide to Lord Alan Sugar on the business reality game show *The Apprentice*, she is currently CEO of the football club that one of this book's authors supports. (West Ham United – did we mention it?)

5

What woman was described as the 'angel of prisons'? Born in 1780 to a prominent Quaker family in Norwich, her mother a member of the Barclay family (as in: the founders of Barclays Bank), she is renowned for being a significant force behind new legislation for the humane treatment of prisoners. The *slightly more* humane treatment of prisoners – she ensured, for example, that those being transported to Australia would be provided with a share of food and water on the voyage. Her face will be familiar to many readers who still prefer cash to contactless cards, as her face was on the reverse of the UK £5 bank note from 2002 to 2017.

6

Writing a blog under a pseudonym for BBC Urdu outlining her life under Taliban occupation in her family's region of Pakistan, who rose to prominence after a *New York Times* documentary about her life? Currently studying for a degree in Philosophy, Politics & Economics at Lady Margaret Hall in Oxford (an *alma mater* of Bobby), she was the youngest person ever to be awarded a Nobel Peace Prize, at the age of 17.

7

Born with the medical condition of *spina bifida* that prevented her from walking and running, who was christened Carys Davina but got her commonly-used nickname from her sister referring to her as 'tiny' upon first seeing her as a baby? With 30 world records to her name and eleven gold medals over four Paralympic Games, she also has six London Marathon winners' medals – her mantelpiece must be overflowing.

8

Because of a thirteenth birthday gift, an autograph book with a red and white chequered cover, what girl has her old residence converted into a museum in Amsterdam? Referring to the diary in early letters as Emmy, Marianne, Conny and Pop, it is most famous for the period in which she was writing to her imaginary friend Kitty. Her older sister Margot Betti had a diary that was sadly never found.

9

Making her professional debut in 1957 as Ophelia in *Hamlet* with the Old Vic Company, which classically trained actress recently impressed in a rap alongside London MC Lethal Bizzle? Despite five Academy Award nominations, her most prominent award is the 1998 Oscar for Best Supporting Actress for her role in *Shakespeare in Love*. Younger readers will know her as 'M', the Head of MI6 in the James Bond films from 1995 to 2012.

10

Who was depicted by Mexican American actress Salma Hayek in a biopic of 2002? In a series of unfortunate events, this woman was left disabled by childhood polio and was then seriously injured aged 18 in a bus accident. Forcibly bedbound, she picked up her father's paintbrush and never looked back. Frequently including monkeys in her paintings, she overtook even the massive artistic reputation of her massive husband, Diego Rivera.

11

Having worked for consultants McKinsey and The World Bank, who became the first woman to get elected to the board at her existing technology company? Joining forces with the likes of Beyoncé, Jennifer Garner and Condoleezza

Rice, she started a campaign to ban the use of the word 'bossy' when talking about girls. Publishing her first book in 2013, *Lean In: Women, Work and the Will to Lead*, she is current Chief Operating Officer of Facebook.

12

At one stage, what woman had a pet baby deer named Pippin that she took with her to supermarkets? Born in 1929 in Belgium, this British actress defined feminine glamour and dignity. She devoted the latter years of her life to humanitarian work with UNICEF, and is renowned for her role in the film adaptation of a short story, the title of which was also used by band Deep Blue Something for their 1993 hit song.

13

'I could feel the crowd all over me. I felt the emotion being absorbed into every pore of my body.' These are the words of which athlete, born in

1973? She rose to global attention by lighting the Olympic flame at the 2000 Sydney Olympics and winning the 400m sprint in an outfit that would look great at a 1970s roller disco event (a green, gold and silver bodysuit).

14

A novelist, poet and lady-in-waiting at the Imperial court during the Heian period of Japanese history, what woman wrote a novel that is compulsory for most Japanese students to study? She is now best known as the most likely author of *The Tale of Genji*, sometimes called the world's first novel or the first novel still to be considered a classic. I sense a Nintendo game in the making...

15

Born surname, Gordon, her mother wanted her to avoid the scandalous Romantic ideals of her father and so had her tutored in maths and science from the age of four. Mentored by the 'father of the computer' Charles Babbage, this woman created the first algorithm to be carried out by a machine and henceforth became the first computer programmer. Yes, when you think 'computer programmer', think of a hoop-skirted and ringleted Victorian lady. Attending at her deathbed, her friend Dickens read to her from his novel *Dombey and Son*. Who was this well-connected woman, the very opposite of a nerd?

16

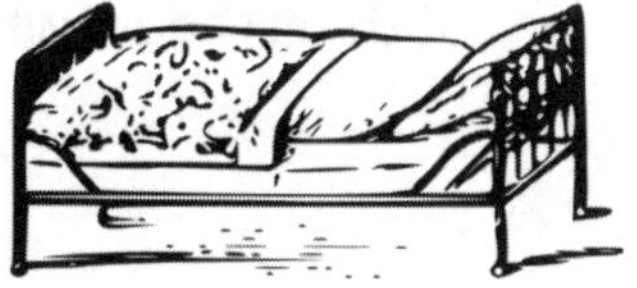

'The news comes between Iraqi weddings being bombed and people dying in the Dominican Republic in flash floods, so we have to get it into perspective'. Part of a group of artists known as the 'Young British Artists' in the late 1980s, these are the words of which British artist, responding to the 2004 fire in east London that destroyed her work *Everyone I Have Ever Slept With 1963-1995*?

17

Born on Christmas Day, this woman was the first person ever to choose the Backstreet Boys as a music choice for BBC Radio Four's *Desert Island Discs*. Truly, a positive role model for our times! However, it is for winning a show that she is famed. After winning, she said 'I'm never gonna say, "I don't think I can." I can and I will.' (Mr Seagull is a proponent of this attitude and encourages his students to think likewise during Maths lessons.) Her first baked item was puff pastry in school, and she has since baked a cake for the Queen's 90th birthday; who is this celebrity baker?

18

Born in 1805 in Jamaica, this woman first visited Britain as a young woman and ran a hotel in Panama. Her reputation rivalled that of Florence Nightingale after the Crimean War, and she is now celebrated for her work in helping the sick and wounded. Voted in 2004 to be the Greatest Black Briton, what woman was largely forgotten for more than a century after her death?

19

Born Gabrielle, she was given her nickname by soldiers in the audience to which she sang onstage. At first designing hats, she introduced the Little Black Dress to 1920s fashion, which was dubbed by French *Vogue* as her 'Ford'. Which French designer is most renowned for her first perfume, named 'No. 5'?

20

US President Truman called her 'First Lady of the World' in tribute to her human rights achievements. Her uncle was the President that the teddy bear was named after. Having once gone flying with the legendary pilot Amelia Earhart, this woman even starred in a margarine commercial – is there no end to her talents? Appointed as a UN delegate in 1946, who was the woman who was a driving force behind the UN's Declaration of Human Rights?

•

CHAPTER 23: 15 OXFORD COLLEGES

We respectfully offer this category to a rival university. The answers to the following questions are also (roughly) the names of colleges at the University of Oxford. Sometimes the spelling is different, and words such as 'College' and 'Hall' are not included in the answers.

1

This East Anglian king reportedly suffered treatment similar to that endured by St Sebastian. According to the Abbot of Fleury, the king refused to submit to the Danes because they would not convert to Christianity. Consequently, the Danes threw spears at him until they pierced him 'like the bristles of a hedgehog'. It is alleged that after he was finally beheaded, his head retained the ability to speak. Who is this king, the subject of veneration after his death?

2

This man had a nickname meaning 'Empty Coat'. He was a claimant to the throne of Scotland, a claim he successfully pursued with the help of Edward I of England. He would later meet with disaster, however, when he refused to support Edward in a war with France. (Isn't that what friends are for?) Edward would consequently take him prisoner and strip him of his title. Which king is referred to here?

3

What name results when the word for sea (in French) is combined with the word for 2,240 pounds (for a Briton) or the word for 2,000 pounds (for an American)?

4

What word can refer to a family of Old World birds as well as several unrelated species in a genus of New World birds? One species of the New World type of this bird, noted for its orange-black colour, is named after the city of Baltimore, Maryland. According to Jared Diamond, some species of the old-world variety located in Australasia mimic friarbirds, and are in turn mimicked by honeyeaters (it's a truism that nothing is original).

5

What name links the following:

- A university attended by Robert Bolt and JK Rowling;
- The location of a notable independent school founded in 1781 in New Hampshire; and
- A book of Anglo-Saxon poetry, containing lines that translate to 'Hail, Earendel, brightest of angels / over middle-earth sent to men'?

Hogwarts, of course, is not a fee-paying school, and yet never seems to get Ofsted inspections – now that's a real fantasy...

6

According to Eliza Doolittle in *My Fair Lady*, hurricanes hardly ever happen in Hereford, Hampshire and what other place, located near the River Lea? The country seat to which she may be referring was once the site of a castle, though very little of the castle remains.

7

What chess opening is an attempt by White to sacrifice a pawn in order to gain control of the centre squares? It is one of the oldest recorded chess openings, and it remains popular today. (HINT: it's not Keith Richards, but it could be described as glam-rock.) It is often referred to as a gambit, even though Black cannot hold its advantage.

8

The final day of the Mexican Día de Muertos coincides with a Christian holiday dedicated to what group of people? These people are collectively the faithful who have died but remain in purgatory to be purified, as opposed to those who are already in heaven (who are commemorated on the previous day). If you happen to have ever been on a flight that's been delayed, you'll know how Purgatory feels.

9

Tycho Brahe (1546-1601) lost a body part in a duel. Subsequently, he wore a prosthetic replacement. The prosthetic was long thought to have been made of silver or gold, but researchers dug up and examined Tycho's body in 2010, to find stains containing copper and zinc. What is it that researchers concluded that Brahe must have worn? We can safely say that his opponent must've been flailing his sword around a bit.

10

This Texan city has a Latin name which comes from the name of the bay on which it is located. The bay in turn was named by a Spanish explorer, who discovered it on a feast day honouring the Sacrament. What city is home to a branch of Texas A&M University and is known as the 'Sparkling City by the Sea'?

11

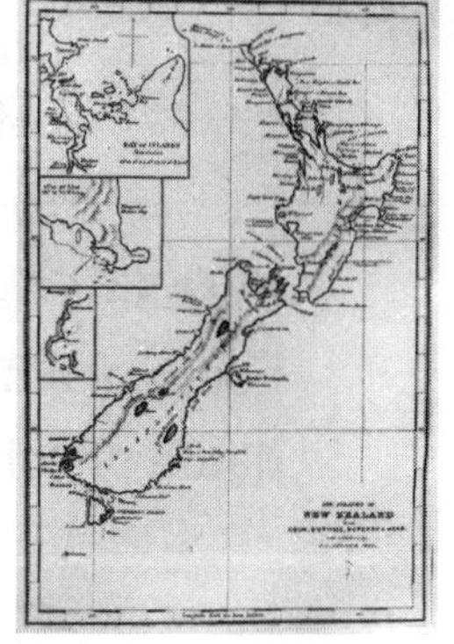

This city is named for Jesus, who must have been quite an urbane tourist judging by the number of cities named for him. It was settled by people known as the 'Canterbury Pilgrims'. It is also known as Ōtautahi. What city is the most populous city on the South Island of New Zealand?

12

These reptiles cannot turn anyone to stone, though they are known as basilisks. What alternate name for a lizard native to the tropics of Central and South America derives from its ability to run across water on its hind legs? It's not 'the waterski lizard'.

13

When one bunches preserved pork into little balls or lumps. (Trust me.)

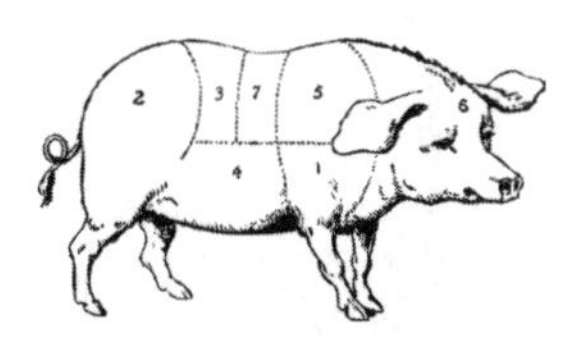

14

Henry VIII created a hereditary peerage for Anne Boleyn as 'Marquesse' of this place, which was also the birthplace of Henry VII. Moreover, the name for this Welsh city is also used in the name of a breed of corgi (HINT: It is also the name of colleges in Cambridge and Brown).

15

This battle was one of the last to take place in the English Civil War. It involved the forces of Oliver Cromwell and an army mostly made up of Scots led by Charles II. Charles lost the battle, eventually fleeing to the continent and according to legend, sleeping in an oak tree along the way. Another English legend is the distinctive fermented fish sauce that was later developed in this city and named after it. What is the city referred to here?

•

CHAPTER 24:
20 6.48 A.M. PUZZLE FOR *TODAY* (AND TOMORROW)

If you happen to tune in around 6.48am on BBC Radio Four, you'll know this is the time for their daily #PuzzleforToday. Bobby and Eric set their first puzzle for listeners on Monday 7th August 2017 and have been regular contributors since, creating brainteasers for listeners to get their cerebral armoury operating (with the Today Programme *getting about 7 million weekly listeners, that's a lot of brain-power being exercised!)*

Sometimes you need the calmness of a monk to methodically take apart a puzzle; other times, you'll need the ferocity of a seagull going after stray chips on Brighton beach. Funnily enough, Mr Seagull's preferred method actually involves giving the mind perhaps 30-45 seconds of calm, freely associative thought, to see if, spirit-like and effortless, the answer will simply descend. Mr Monkman, in contrast, usually takes a systematic approach to the problem. On one particular broadcast, Eric asked Bobby to explain the technical, mathematical difference between the words 'combination' and 'permutation'. A listener subsequently edited

the Wikipedia page for 'combination lock' to read:
"Bobby Seagull, star of University Challenge*, has pointed out that, mathematically, the name is incorrect, as a combination allows reordering of the elements. The better name would be 'permutation lock', since the order matters."*
This is because if you tried to undo a bicycle combination lock with a code of 1234 with 1243 it would not unlock, as it requires the correct permutation *of the code. Mr Seagull will be contacting Halfords and Argos in the near future to get them to correct the category classification to 'permutation lock'.*
This section involves some puzzles previously tried out on a radio audience, and some fresh new ones devised to fiendishly test your minds...

1

1 = Vietnam, 2 = Panama, 3 = Burundi, 4 = New Zealand, 5 = People's Republic of China.
What is 6?

2

France is Marseille, Germany is Hamburg, Italy is Milan, Spain is Barcelona.
What is the UK?

3

The main draw for the Wimbledon men's or women's tennis championship has 128 entrants. If we quadrupled the number of entrants in the draw to 512, how many matches would there have to be in the traditional knockout format for there to be a winner?

4

1 = Spain
2 = Turkey
3 = Canada
4 = Uzbekistan
What is 5?

5

2, 2, 1, 5, 11, 12, 4, 1, 6, 3, 2, 10, 2, 1, 4, 7, 4, 2, 2, 4, 2, 1.

What is the next number?
(HINT: [Perhaps necessary!] Channel your inner Jane Austen, as you will have to swallow your pride and show no opening prejudice or bias when attempting to answer this.)

6

5 = Stockholm, 10 = Los Angeles, 15 = Helsinki, 20 = Munich, 25 = Barcelona.
What is 30?

7

Take a journey on the London Underground using the following lines in this particular order: Central, London Overground, Circle, District, Piccadilly. Why might a History (or Science) teacher feel this journey is incomplete?

8

It happened in the beginning and the second time. It then happened again on the eighth time. It then happened on the tenth and eleventh time and it most recently happened on the 16th time. It appears highly unlikely it will happen again on the 21st time in 2018. What are we referring to?

9

Let's take a step across the pond that is the Atlantic Ocean and look at the United States. Hiram, Stephen, Thomas, John, James and William are part of an exclusive, and perhaps slightly less official, American club. What connects them?

10

Let's engage your mind for numbers. What is next in this sequence: 3, 4, 6, 8, 12, 14, 18, 20?

11

If 6 = South Africa, 5 = Guyana, 4 = Malaysia, 3 = Belgium, 2 = Nigeria, why would we have had an answer to 1 back in 2011 but no longer now?

12

If you're not as avid a listener as us to the BBC Radio Four *Today Programme* (and why not? I might ask), you might need to check out who the presenters of the *Today Programme* are for this question. If Mishal is 9, Andrew is 10, and both Sarah and Justin are 11, what is John?

13

Why might the residents of 5, 7, 10, 24, 55 and 1600 pay a visit to number 760?

14

What connects Ecuador, East Timor, El Salvador, Marshall Islands, Micronesia, Palau, Turks and Caicos, British Virgin Islands and Zimbabwe?

15

What is the next animal in the sequence: Sheep, pig, rabbit, monkey, ox, snake, rooster, tiger, sheep?

(HINT: You may want to use a lifeline here and give a phone call to Professor John Curtice from the University of Strathclyde in his capacity as a politics expert.)

16

What is next in this sequence: C, W, G, C H, A, B, E, ...?

17

Bobby is a particular fan of the Ella Fitzgerald and Louis Armstrong version of the song 'Let's Call The Whole Thing Off'. The couple have differences in pronunciations of words such as 'potato', 'tomato' and 'pyjama'. Let's look at a difference between us British and our US neighbours across the Pond. For the Brits cotton, for the Yanks paper. For the Brits sugar, for the Yanks iron. For the Brits salt, for the Yanks bronze. For the Brits copper, for the Yanks pottery. What are we talking about?

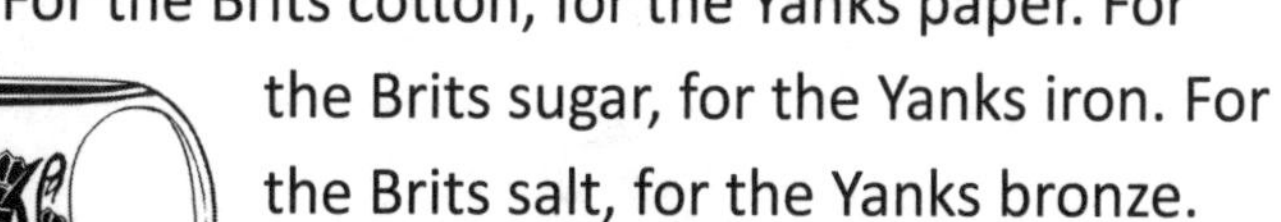

18

234, 4916, 82764.
What is the next number?

19

What is next in the sequence: O, O, T, T, F, E, T, T, T, F, E, ...?

20

The United States of America, Cyprus, France, Germany and Poland are part of an exclusive club. Why was Japan admitted into this club in 2016? If this club had a patron, it might be Dmitri Mendeleev.

•

DIFFERENT FORMS OF QUIZ

Monkman and Seagull aren't just all about University Challenge, *you know. There doesn't need to be a buzzer for it to be fun. To be a true polymath, you must be aware of the need to test yourself in many different ways.*

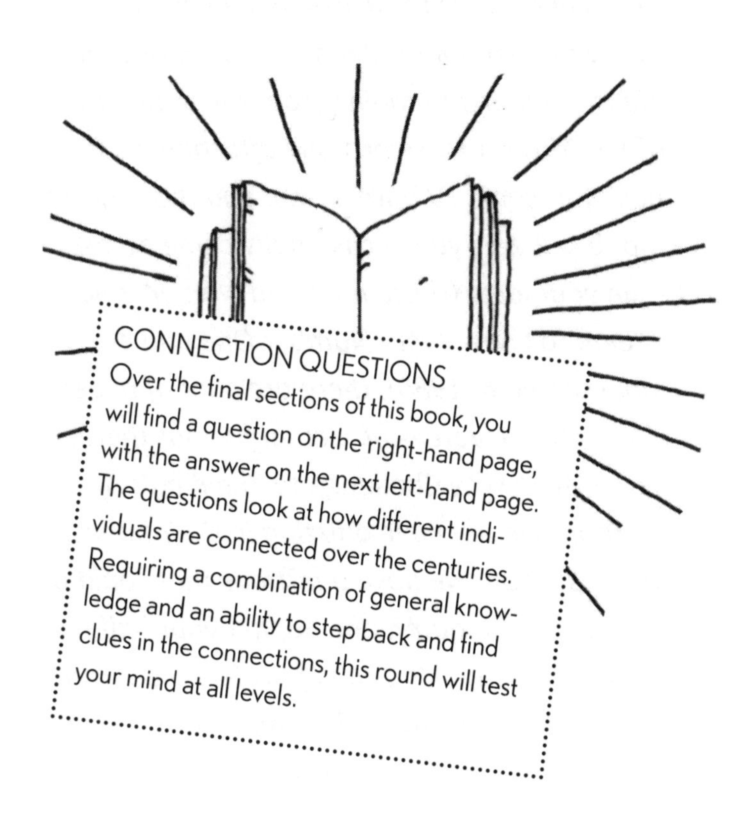

CHAPTER 25: 48 PUB QUIZ

Fish and chips, the Queen, Wimbledon, the Beatles, talking about the weather in a queue – all quintessential features of Britishness. It would not be stretching truth to add the noble art of Pub Quizzing to that list.

Eric and Bobby took part in a pub quiz for their BBC Radio Four programme Monkman & Seagull's Polymathic Adventure *but were not able to convert their (not-so) trivial University Challenge skills to success in a new format. They missed out on the medal positions and finished fourth! Judging from the popularity of* The Times *Crossword, the affection we Brits have for iconic TV quiz shows, and those great pub-quizzers you occasionally come across in your local (those men and women who seem to know every Number One and every goal scored in 1985), there are a lot of hugely talented devotees of factual fun out there. From* University Challenge *to The King's Arms, Britons clearly have quizzing in their bones.*

In this section, we have questions that could be used for a pub quiz night. So, get your half pint of bitter (Seagull's drink of preference), from your fridge or from the bar, and let the games commence!

1

What surname is shared by the British actress renowned for her recurring role as Magda in the BBC sitcom *Absolutely Fabulous*, the partner-in-crime of Edinburgh graverobber William Hare, and the Anglo-Irish politician known for his support for the American revolution?

2

In a 2016 public poll, the British showed their quirky good humour by voting to choose the name *'Boaty McBoatface'* for a research vessel. In honour of a British naturalist, what name replaced this?

3

First entering orbit around Saturn in 2004, what space probe named after an Italian scientist made its 'Grand Finale' by crashing into the gas giant in September 2017?

CONNECTION 1. The year of this man's birth was determined, likely incorrectly, by Dionysius Exiguus. According to one account of his life, he was born when Cyrenus (likely Publius Sulpicius Quirinius) was Governor of Syria. This man spent some of his early life in Egypt before moving to a town that is now in northern Israel. Who, upon being asked whether he was King of the Jews, replied with insouciance, 'Thou sayest it'?

4

The surprise TV hit of summer 2017 was the reality dating show *Love Island* on ITV2. Sharing his surname with an alloy of silver, which comedian's narration of the series became as iconic as the contestants themselves?

5

The BBC broadcasts Christmas carols from which Cambridge University college on Christmas Eve each year? Alumni include first Prime Minister of Great Britain Robert Walpole; mathematician code-breaker Alan Turing; novelist Zadie Smith.

6

British band Radiohead released a song called 'Myxomatosis (Judge, Jury & Executioner)' on their 2003 album *Hail to the Thief*. Myxomatosis was introduced into Australia in 1950 in an attempt to control the species of what animal?

ANSWER 1 *Jesus Christ.*

7

The Physical Impossibility of Death in the Mind of Someone Living is a 14-foot tiger shark immersed in formaldehyde in a clear display tank. Which wealthy English artist created this?

8

In July 2017, England beat India in the ICC Women's Cricket World Cup final in part due to the performance of a lifetime by which bowler? Her stunning spell of six for 46 was England's best World Cup bowling figures.

9

More than 300 girls born in England and Wales in 2016 were named Arya, and 69 were named Khaleesi. These are both names from which fantasy drama TV series?

CONNECTION 2. Jesus is mentioned in this man's *Antiquities of the Jews*. This man led the Jewish defenders of Jotapata in a failed attempt to resist a Roman siege. His life was spared following the fall of the city. He was eventually given Roman citizenship and became an historian. Who wrote, alongside *Antiquities of the Jews*, *The Jewish War* and an autobiography?

10

In which 1989 film does the inspirational English teacher John Keating, played by Robin

Williams, ask his students to 'make your lives extraordinary'? He summarises this with the Latin phrase '*carpe diem*'.

11

Believed to have originated from Eton College, the Eton Mess is a traditional English dessert consisting of a mixture of broken meringue, whipped heavy cream and which fruit?

12

William Shatner, Patrick Stewart, Avery Brooks, Kate Mulgrew, Scott Bakula and Chris Pine all star as captains on which American franchise?

13

What animal mascot became the breakaway star at the 2017 World Athletics Championships in London? The collective noun for a group of this kind of animals is an 'array'.

ANSWER 2 *Josephus (or Titus Flavius Josephus; or Yosef ben Matityahu)* – **Christianity mentioned by Josephus.**

14

'Where is Love?', 'As Long As He Needs Me' and 'Consider Yourself' are songs from which British musical film of 1968, directed by Carol Reed and winner of six Academy Awards?

15

Leeds Castle, which Henry VIII used as a residence for his first wife Katherine of Aragon, is in which English county?

16

Demis Hassabis co-founded 'DeepMind', a London-based, machine learning, Artificial Intelligence start-up. Since being acquired by Google, it created a computer programme that defeated Lee Sedol, the world champion in which game?

CONNECTION 3. This man, the commander of the Roman forces at Jotapata, spared Josephus' life. Josephus later claims to have told this man he would someday become Emperor of Rome. If so, Josephus' prediction was correct. This man came out on top as the last emperor standing in 69 AD, known as the Year of the Four Emperors. He began construction of the Colosseum. Who gives his name to a French edifice for public urinals, in reference to his taxing of urine collected from a public sewer, used (among other things) to get ammonia for whitening clothing?

17

Although One Direction are probably the most popular

act to have sprung from the reality music show *The X Factor*, they came third in 2010. Which solo artist won?

18

A Vindication of the Rights of Woman (1792) is the work of which English philosopher? Her logic was fearsome, but her daughter's power to terrify lay in the realm of the imagination – she authored the gothic novel *Frankenstein*.

19

What is the name of the 2017 Netflix documentary by Bryan Fogel that exposed a major doping scandal in Russia? It shares its title with a character from Greek mythology, the son of the creator of Minos' Labyrinth.

20

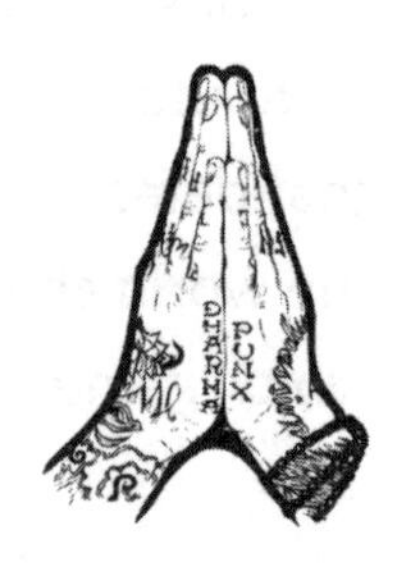

Born Michael Owuo, which English grime and hip hop artist made the first grime album to reach Number One in the UK Albums Charts? The album is *Gang Signs & Prayer*; the artist's most successful song is 'Shut Up'.

ANSWER 3 *Vespasian (or Titus Flavius Vespasianius; or Caesar Vespasianus Augustus)* - **Josephus prophesied about Vespasian.**

21

Graduating with a BSc in Mathematics from Sussex University in 1966, who was the last English woman to win Wimbledon, back in 1977?

22

Master of Emmanuel College, Cambridge, Dame Fiona Reynolds, was former Director General of which conservation organisation? Founded in 1895, this charity's purpose is to preserve and protect historic places and spaces, forever, for everyone.

23

'This Is It' was the name of a series of 50 concerts, from July 2009 to March 2010, planned by Michael Jackson at which venue? Due to be his first major concert series since 1997, Jackson died three weeks before the first performance.

CONNECTION 4. This man was a consul alongside Vespasian when the latter was emperor. This man would himself become emperor after Vespasian's son Domitian. He began his reign with a promise not to execute any Roman senators. Cassius Dio praises his modesty, his economy and his generosity. In spite of these qualities (or perhaps because of them), his reign was marked by a revolt by the Praetorian Guard. Apparently he did not pay them enough. Who survived this revolt, adopting Trajan as his successor?

24

Oxford University, the Royal Engineers and Old Etonians were among the first winners in the 1870s of which sports tournament?

25

The 1984 film *Amadeus* depicts a fictional Wolfgang Amadeus Mozart. However the film's anti-hero was Italian composer Antonio Salieri, who was acted by which American actor? He won an Academy Award for Best Actor in this role.

ANSWER 4 Nerva (or Marcus Cocceius Nerva) - **Under Vespasian, Nerva was consul.**

26

The tetrahedron, the cube, the octahedron, the dodecahedron and the icosahedron are regular, convex solids named after which ancient Greek philosopher?

27

The Basilica of Our Lady of Peace of Yamoussoukro is listed by the Guinness World Records as the largest 'church' in the world, overtaking St Peter's Basilica in the Vatican. Which African country is this in?

28

Solid, liquid, gas are three of the four fundamental states of matter. Meaning 'mouldable substance' or 'jelly' in ancient Greek, what is the fourth one?

29

Born in Singapore, which BAFTA-winning English documentary filmmaker and broadcaster is best known for series such as *Weird Weekends* and his BBC Two specials?

30

On which country's national flag is there an emblem known as the Ashoka Chakra? This is a wheel with 24 spokes.

31

The 2015 Man Booker Prize winner was *A Brief History of Seven Killings* by Marlon James. This novel covers several decades and explores the attempted assassination of which musician in 1976?

32

Peter Preston from 1975 to 1995, Alan Rusbridger from 1995 to 2015 and currently Katharine Viner. These are editors of which national newspaper, originally founded in Manchester in 1821?

33

Sir Richard Evans, former President of Wolfson College, Cambridge, is renowned for writing the three-volume *The Third Reich Trilogy,* charting the rise and collapse of Nazi Germany. British actor John Sessions depicts Sir Richard in which 2016 film, a historical drama starring Rachel Weisz and Timothy Spall?

34

What five-letter Danish and Norwegian word can roughly be translated as 'cosiness' and comes from a Norwegian word meaning 'feeling of wellbeing'?

35

'Draco Dormiens Numquam Titillandus' is the motto of which Scottish boarding school?

36

The Royal Institution Christmas Lectures have inspired both children and adults on scientific topics since 1825. Though he did not present the first lectures, which English scientist initiated this series? He was on the reverse of the £20 note from 1991 to 2001.

37

Chariots of Fire is a film of 1981, adapted from the story of two athletes in the 1924 Olympics. Although the phrase 'chariots of fire' is an original title, which poet's lines inspired the phrase?

CONNECTION 5. Nerva was the first of the 'Five Good Emperors'. This man was the last. He was emperor during a plague that killed many Romans, likely including his co-emperor Lucius Verus. Roman military successes against the Marcomanni, Quadi and Sarmations are commemorated by a column named for this man. While he was on campaign, this man, also a philosopher, wrote some of his Meditations. What man was succeeded as emperor by his son Commodus?

38

A lifelong fan of Norwich City football club, who has published *The Stars' Tennis Balls*, (a modern retelling of *The Count of Monte Cristo*) and a guide to writing poetry, *The Ode Less Travelled: Unlocking the Poet Within*? He also starred in BBC sitcom *Blackadder*.

39

To the nearest five years, how long is the Hundred Years War between England and France traditionally considered to have lasted?

40

The scientific name of the house mouse is *Mus musculus*. What organism has the scientific name *Balenoptera musculus*?

41

Zagazig, Ismailia and Port Said are all cities in which African country?

ANSWER 5 *Marcus Aurelius (or Marcus Aurelius Antoninus Augustus)* - **Nerva was the first of the five good emperors. Marcus Antonius Aurelius was the last.**

42

Ra's al-Ghul, translated as 'The Head of the Ogre' is the Arabic name of a particular star in what constellation, associated with a figure famous for cutting off a ghoulish head? These days, many stars are referred to by catalogue number – a little less romantic than the ancient naming system.

43

China has land borders with 14 countries. Two of these countries have land borders with only three other countries (including China). One is Vietnam. What is the other?

44

Since 1970, the Bank of England has featured historical figures on its banknotes. As of 2017, which figure featured on a note was born most recently (not including the Queen)? For an extra point, which figure featured on a note was born the earliest?

45

The Toronto Maple Leafs are a Canadian ice hockey team. In which year, significant to Canada, did they last win the Stanley Cup (as of 2017)? Our Montreal-born editor Todd prefers The Habs.

46

There are two plays by Anton Chekhov with the name of a bird in their common English title. Name one of them.

47

'[J]am to-morrow and jam yesterday – but never jam to-day' is a quote from a work by which author?

48

In theatre, what metaphorical object, sometimes broken, is said to separate performers from the audience?

•

CHAPTER 26:
10 NEWSPAPER QUIZ

The 'newspaper quiz', daily or weekly, is a household institution. Unlike the pub quiz, doing the newspaper quiz is a family-friendly activity, often associated with festive gatherings or just quiet Sundays spent together. Try it yourself – you may be surprised at the specialities of your nearest and dearest.

Equally possible, and less competitive: do the newspaper quiz whilst sitting at your kitchen table, with a cup of coffee, by yourself.

1

Swahili and Zulu belong to which language family, the proto-variety of which is believed to have originated in Western Africa?

2

Which film, directed by Hayao Miyazaki and produced by Studio Ghibli, won the award for Best Animated feature at the 75th Academy Awards, held in 2003?

CONNECTION 6. A bronze statue of Marcus Aurelius stands in the Capitoline Museum in Rome. Allegedly, it was saved from being melted down like many statues of pagan emperors because it was mistaken for a statue of another man, the subject of this question. (They must have shared a Roman nose.) This man triumphed over Maxentius at the Battle of the Milvian Bridge. Who was the first Christian emperor of Rome?

3

'*Lachrimae Pavan*' (in sung form known as 'Flow, My Tears') and 'Come Again, Sweet Love Doth Now Invite' are pieces of music by which English Renaissance composer?

4

W^+, W^- and Z^0, massive particles known as intermediate vector bosons (to their closest friends) mediate which fundamental physical force?

5

The University of Wittenberg (now the Martin Luther University of Halle-Wittenberg) claims two of the most famous characters of literature as attendees. One was the titular character in a play by William Shakespeare, and the other likewise in a play by Christopher Marlowe. Who are they?

ANSWER 6 *Constantine I (or Constantine the Great; or Flavius Valerius Aurelius Constantinus Augustus)* - **Marcus Aurelius' statue was mistaken for that of Constantine the Great.**

6

Dunedin (or Ōtepoti) and Nelson (or Whakatū) are cities located on what island?

7

Which British head of state died at age 85, even though he ruled England, Scotland and Ireland for less than one year?

8

Alfred Marshall and William Stanley Jevons are academics now associated with which field of knowledge?

9

Epistemology is a Greek term that is used to describe the study of what?

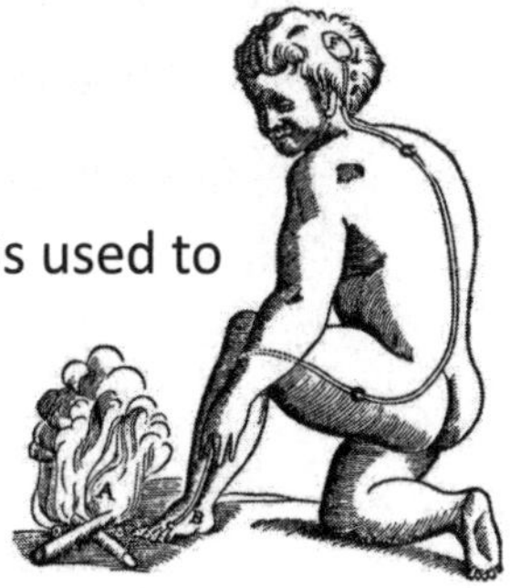

10

Which Canadian university was founded in 1821 following a donation from the will of a fur trader (he is described as 'a native of Glasgow North Britain' on his monument)?

CHAPTER 27: 50 PRIMARY SCHOOL-LEVEL QUESTIONS

To inculcate young brains into the fiendish world of quizzing, here is a section that should ('should' being the key word) ease younger readers into the fun of facts. As Bobby is also a secondary school Maths teacher, he has put on his teacher hat as Mr Seagull for this section (joined by Mr Monkman, of course, as well). We have pored over the UK National Curriculum for Key Stage 2 – so (in theory) what an 11-year-old will have covered at primary school – and used that as inspiration for setting these questions.

If you're an 11-year-old, let's see how much attention you've been paying to your teachers. If you're an adult, don't skip past these questions – can you beat an 11-year-old?!

HISTORY

1

Older than Stonehenge and possibly your grandparents, known as the 'Scottish Pompeii', what is the name of Europe's most complete Neolithic village? This UNESCO World Heritage site and stone-built settlement is located on the Bay of Skaill on the west coast of mainland Scotland.

2

Whilst it was arguably a gradual process, the Roman conquest of Britain was effectively begun in AD 43 under which Emperor? He was the first Roman Emperor to be born outside Italy. (Earlier invasions of Britain by Caesar and Caligula's failed attempts are not included).

CONNECTION 7. The 'Donation of Constantine' is a forged document, purporting to give large portions of Constantine's empire to the Roman Church. It was likely created to serve as a precedent for King Pepin the Short to transfer control of the Papal States to the Church. Pepin the Short was the father of the man who is the subject of this question, who was himself sometimes called *Pater Europae*, or 'Father of Europe'. He controlled territory in what is now Italy, France and Germany. Who employed the Englishman Alcuin as a scholar and teacher?

ANSWER 7 *Charlemagne (or Charles I; or Charles the Great; or Karl der Grosse)* – **Constantine made a donation that was used by Pepin the Short, father of Charlemagne.**

3

The son of Ethelred II 'The Unready', what is the name of the penultimate Anglo-Saxon king of England? He became king in 1042, reigning until his death on 4th January 1066 (and only had to wait 900 years for England to win the Football World Cup). He was buried in the abbey he had constructed at Westminster.

4

Initially discovered by a French engineer who noticed a slab of granite sticking out of the ground, what item was captured by the British and has been the source of many a selfie at the British Museum since 1802, as the most visited object there?

5

Taking the throne on 15th January 1559, who was monarch of England and Ireland until their death in 1603? This monarch's mother was Anne Boleyn (who lost her head after Henry VIII had a bad day. I bet she was mad). She often wore white make-up made of lead – a substance thick enough to cover up scars left from a bout of smallpox.

6

Born in London in 1955, what is the name of the man credited with inventing the World Wide Web? Having also created the first web browser and editor, this man was seen on the stage of the Opening Ceremony of the London 2012 Olympics with the message 'This is for everyone'.

7

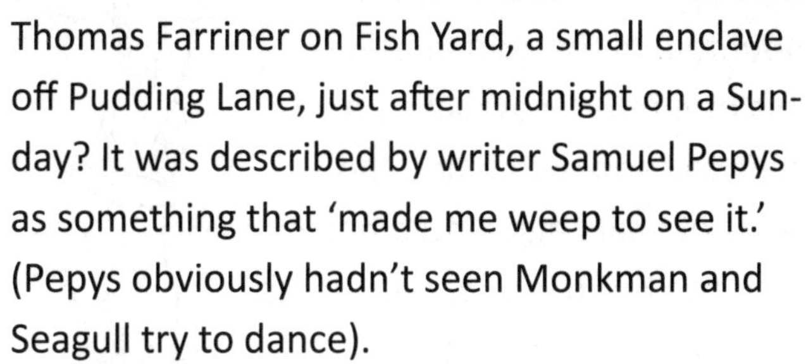

What event of British national significance started at the bakery of Thomas Farriner on Fish Yard, a small enclave off Pudding Lane, just after midnight on a Sunday? It was described by writer Samuel Pepys as something that 'made me weep to see it.' (Pepys obviously hadn't seen Monkman and Seagull try to dance).

8

What is the name of the pre-Columbian American civilisation that developed in the areas around modern day Mexico and Central America? Despite existing for more than 2,000 years and developing the science of astronomy, a calendar system and hieroglyphic writing, they saw a terminal decline in their civilisation – no one is quite sure why.

•

GEOGRAPHY

1

Standing at 1,344m tall in the western end of the Grampian Mountains, what is the highest mountain in the British Isles? This mountain is actually an ancient volcano, and many thousands of years ago would have been too hot to scale, despite its location in dreich Scotland.

2

Like a giant lightsabre lighting up Greenwich Park at night, what is the name of the path that is lit by a green laser at the Royal Observatory in London?

3

If you happen to use a physical map in the UK (unlikely now, thanks to Google Maps), it is likely that they are produced by this national mapping agency which covers the island of Great Britain. What is the name of this agency, whose name indicates its original military purpose?

4

Major ones include the Pacific, North American and Eurasian, and minor ones include Somali, Nazca and Caribbean. Generally around 100km thick, and consisting of oceanic and continental crust, what is the name given to pieces of the Earth's crust

CONNECTION 8. This man gave Charlemagne an elephant and a water clock as gifts. Not exactly appropriate for the mantelpiece. He ruled an empire stretching from Africa to central Asia, first from Baghdad and later from Raqqa. His reign was considered a golden age and was later memorialised in fiction. Indeed, this man appeared as a character in some of the stories of the One Thousand-and-One Arabian Nights. However, he did not lead an entirely charmed life. Which fifth Abbasid caliph ordered the execution of his friend and vizier Ja'far?

and uppermost mantle? It is not advisable to stand on one of these when they're upset. Literally upset, that is.

ANSWER 8 Harun al-Rashid - **Charlemagne received an elephant from Harun al-Rashid.**

5

If you're on the hunt for fantastic beasts and where to find them, you could do worse than heading to this country, home to komodo dragons, orangutans, Javan rhinoceroses and leopards. Ranking after China, India and the United States, what is currently the fourth most populated country in the world, with approximately 260 million people?

6

Only four countries (Lesotho, New Zealand, Swaziland and Uruguay – not such a bad football World Cup line-up) lie entirely south of this imaginary line. What is the name of the line of latitude going around the Earth at approximately 23.5 degrees south of the equator?

MATHS

1

If an isosceles triangle has one angle of 40 degrees, what are the other two missing angles? Bonus point if you can spell 'isosceles'.

2

A coordinate grid can be called a Cartesian coordinate system. A French mathematician came up with the system whilst lying in bed, when he saw a spider crawling from the ceiling and realised its position could be determined by its distance from the edges. What is the name of this mathematician? And why didn't he just run away screaming?

3

There are twice as many students who prefer Beyoncé to Taylor Swift in a primary school. With the total number of students at 480, how many students preferred Taylor Swift? Now look what you've made me do, going about mixing popular chart music with numbers.

4

You take a pizza, and slice it in half. Then slice both halves up into thirds. Then slice up each of the new thirds into quarters. You will now have how many slices, for how many impatient friends?

5

Face northwards, turn a quarter turn to the right, then a half turn to the left, then three quarters to the right, then a half turn to the left and then three quarter turn to the right. Unless you've fallen over dizzy, in which direction are you facing?

6

You give your sunflower plant plenty of milk to drink (if it's good enough for babies, it's good enough for the sunflowers, I say) and it grows in height at a rate of 10% every year.
If you start at 1m tall, how tall is the plant after two years?

ENGLISH

1

'The quick brown fox jumps over the lazy dog' is a sentence that contains all the letters of the alphabet. Meaning 'every letter' in Greek, what is the word for this linguistic trick? You can say this word by combining the 'surname' of the character of the boy who never grows up and the single unit that is one thousandth of the weight of a usual bag of sugar.

2

Perhaps the oldest surviving long poem in Old English, what epic poem produced about a thousand years ago follows a Scandinavian hero, who slays a monster called Grendel, and Grendel's mother for good measure? Seamus Heaney, the great Irish poet, published a version of this poem.

3

'Malayalam' is the name of the language spoken in Kerala, India. 'Madam I'm Adam' are possibly the first words spoken by Adam to Eve. 'A man, a plan, a canal, Panama' might describe the process of building the Panama canal. These are all examples of words or phrases that can be read the same backwards as forwards. What is this called? It was coined by Ben Jonson, the English playwright and friend of Shakespeare – not the similarly-named 100m sprinter from 1988 – who ran into trouble.

4

What distinctive presentational feature is shared by the authors of *Winnie-the-Pooh, the Chronicles of Narnia, the Lord of the Rings* and *Harry Potter*? The answer is a bit more challenging than the fact that they write books!

5

'Peter Piper picked a peck of pickled peppers'. Now try saying that again, and then again with a hot pepper in your mouth for added zing. The first phrase is an example of what stylistic literary device, identified by the repeated sound of the first letter in a series of multiple words?

6

Dylan Thomas the major Welsh poet's *Under Milk Wood* describes 'the shops in mourning'. 'Mourning' can be heard as 'mourning' or 'morning'. What is the name of this linguistic feature, a term used to describe words that sound the same but have different meanings? You may want to consider whether you'd rather your doctor lost his 'patients' or his 'patience'!

•

SCIENCE

1

From its discovery in 1930 by Clyde Tombaugh until 2006, Pluto was classified as a regular planet in the Kuiper belt. Just to annoy those who had used mnemonics to memorise the order of the planets at school (such as 'My Very Easy Method Just Speeds Up Naming Planets'), Pluto was re-classified as what type of celestial object, neither a planet nor a natural satellite?

CONNECTION 9. This man was a scholar in Baghdad's House of Wisdom, which was founded by Harun al-Rashid and expanded by his son and successor. 'House of Wisdom' is no idle boast – one of this man's works describes the mathematical system of 'al-jebr', or the putting together of broken parts (today, the system is known as 'algebra'). What man's name, in a modified form, has come to refer to a set of steps that can be used to solve a problem? Because we are kind, just the name given to the set of steps is sufficient.

2

No peeking at your garden for this question. When looking at the carpel, the female part of a flower, this is comprised of three components: the ovary and the style are two of them. What is the name of the sticky surface where the pollen lands, which is supported by the style? No relation to Harry Styles, whose headline group One Direction supports nobody.

3

Leonardo, Donatello, Raphael and the pizza-loving Michelangelo are the crime fighting Teenage Mutant Ninja Turtles. Turtles belong to a species of the order *Testudines*, which is characterised by a special bony shell developing out of their ribs (sounds painful!) which acts to shield their innards (just like Captain America's shield, but part of their body...). Along with crocodiles and snakes, what scientific classification of vertebrates do these *testudines* belong to?

ANSWER 9 *Al-Khwarizmi (or Abu Ja'far Muhammad ibn Musa al-Khwarizmi). Algorithm is also acceptable, as it comes from al-Khwarizmi -* ***Harun al-Rashid's son expanded the House of Wisdom where Al-Khawrizmi worked.***

4

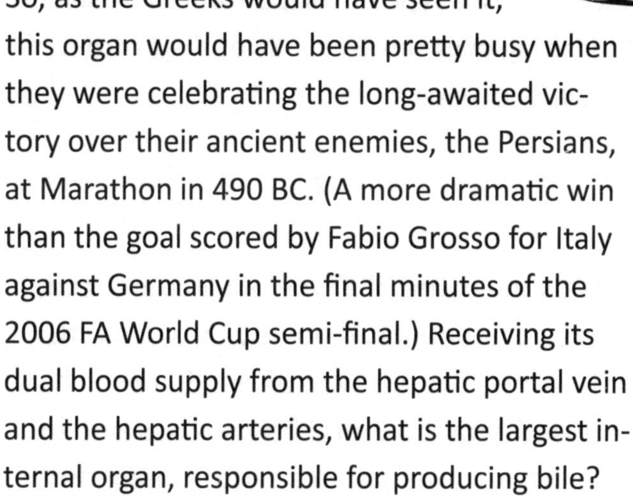

This organ of the human body was considered by the Ancient Greeks to be the home of all human emotions. So, as the Greeks would have seen it, this organ would have been pretty busy when they were celebrating the long-awaited victory over their ancient enemies, the Persians, at Marathon in 490 BC. (A more dramatic win than the goal scored by Fabio Grosso for Italy against Germany in the final minutes of the 2006 FA World Cup semi-final.) Receiving its dual blood supply from the hepatic portal vein and the hepatic arteries, what is the largest internal organ, responsible for producing bile?

5

If you have a sensitive stomach, look away now. When you go upside down in a roller coaster in a loop-the-loop, you might expect to fall out, but a special force keeps you in your seat. What is the name of this force?

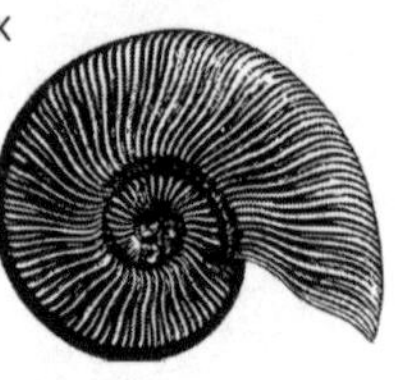

6

Fossils (some of your older teachers?) are often found in what particular type of rock? Chalk, sandstone and limestone all belong to this classification. This type of rock is formed by layers depositing over time, usually at the bottom of lakes and oceans.

7

What is the name of a type of electric circuit, where components are joined by wires with no branches? In this type of circuit, not to be confused with the brutal fitness-class kind of circuit that leaves you in a sweaty heap, the current through each of the components is the same. (HINT: if you have a Netflix account, you might be hooked on one of these.)

8

What is the name of the transition phase in which liquids turn into gas? Two of the most familiar types of this phase include evaporation and boiling. For *Star Trek* fans out there, this answer may be the cause of death, if someone has gotten a bit carried away when using their phasers on 'stun'.

9

Water + carbon dioxide results in sugar (though not the sort you'd put in your tea) and oxygen. This simple equation is the process of photosynthesis, which allows plants to use energy from sunlight to produce sugar, which cellular respiration converts into ATP (nothing to do with the tennis tournament circuit dominated by Federer and Nadal). What is the name of the parts of plant cells where photosynthesis is located?

•

MUSIC

1

The BBC's primary school initiative aims to inspire children to enjoy classical music with ten specially selected pieces of music.

CONNECTION 10. Adelard of Bath translated the works of Al-Khwarizmi into Latin. Adelard of Bath was in turn an inspiration to this other English scientist and mathematician. This later scientist studied at Oxford, and carried out early optical experiments. He is also known for his research into alchemy and other esoteric pursuits. According to legend, he created a 'brazen head' that could speak. What scientist, who shared a surname with a later (seventeenth-century) scientist, is credited as the first European to describe how to make gunpowder?

One of these is by Gustav Holst, a former teacher and director of music at St Paul's Girls' School (so that's 'Mr Holst' to you kids). Having been introduced to astrology by a friend, he composed his suite entitled *The Planets*. Which 'Planet' was written in anticipation of World War One and performed immediately after the war in 1918?

2

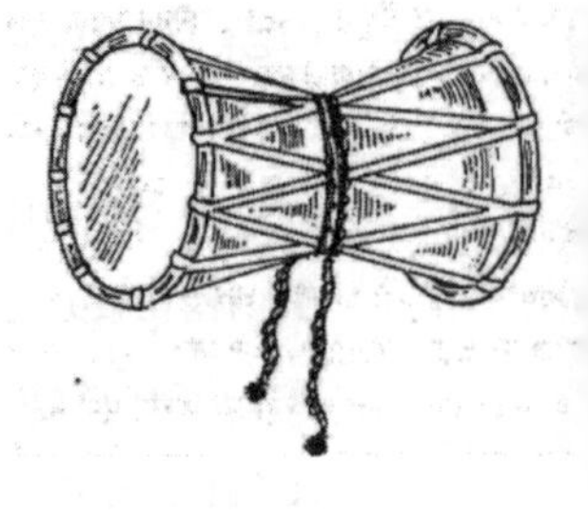

What form of vocal percussion mainly involves the skill of mimicking drum machines solely using the performer's mouth, lips, tongue and voice? Often referred to as 'the fifth element' of hip hop, the name of this type of music may suggest battling it out with gloves (like Muhammad Ali) but, alas, there will only be bruised egos when top British practitioners of this art form such as Beardyman and Shlomo go toe-to-toe.

3

If you want to get your neighbours to move house quickly (or perhaps break your windows in frustration),

ANSWER 10 *Roger Bacon* - ***Adelard of Bath, whose writings influenced Roger Bacon, translated Al-Khwarizi.***

you could do worse than playing this type of musical instrument as a means of persuasion. What is the name of the section of the orchestra in front of the percussion area, that includes trumpets, trombones and tubas? An exotic type of this instrument is the Australian didgeridoo (try getting one of these in your suitcase).

•

ART, DESIGN & TECHNOLOGY

1

Derived from the French word for 'to glue', what artistic technique involved artwork being made from a collection of different forms, creating a new whole? Often an excuse to upset your parents by leaving a mess of cut-up newspaper and magazine clippings on your table, this term was coined by Cubist pioneers Pablo Picasso and his lesser known pal Georges Braque (be honest kids, you haven't heard of him).

2

At 70 metres long and 50 centimetres tall, what embroidered cloth would perhaps make a great cover for a very, very long (and very narrow) dining table? Described by Charles Dickens as 'the work of amateurs' (not a generous man!) and featuring an appearance of Halley's comet, this embroidery was once confiscated during the French Revolution and shows an arrow sticking out of Harold Godwinson's eye (he should have gone to Specsavers).

3

'Give me a place to stand, and I shall move the earth' claimed the ancient Greek mathematician Archimedes in demonstrating the principle of what simple machine? (Though I'm not sure I'd trust a man who forgot to put on his clothes after leaping out of his bath, and ran naked through town shouting 'Eureka'.) Common examples of this mechanism include the crowbar, wheelbarrow and a pair of tweezers.

•

RELIGION

1

Central to this religion is the belief in a supreme God, Brahma, who is worshipped in a variety of forms including Vishnu, Krishna, Rama and Shiva. With about 900 million followers worldwide, what religion originating from India dates back over 2,500 years? If you haven't had the chance, get involved with this religion's festival of Holi in the spring: like a massive pillow fight but one where everyone throws lots of powdered paint and coloured water on each other!

2

Thou shalt have no other gods before me. Thou shalt not commit murder. Thou shalt not use the Lord's name in vain. Thou shalt not use thy mobile phone whilst at the dinner table with thy parents. These (well, most of them) are parts of the Ten Commandments, given to Moses on which biblical mountain?

3

Believed to have lived between the sixth and fourth centuries BC (he wasn't 200 years old, scholars are just not exactly sure about the dates!), what primary figure in a world religion was born in Lumbini in modern day Nepal? To achieve enlightenment, this person sat under a fig tree and meditated until he transcended suffering. He is also known as Siddhartha Gautama.

•

MODERN FOREIGN LANGUAGES

1

What is the name of the stretch of water that separates southern England from northern France? Swimming from England to France is quicker than the other direction (due to the enticing smell of hot croissants wafting across to the

UK). The French call it 'La Manche', meaning 'the sleeve' because of this body of water's long thin shape – like the sleeve of your jumper.

2

In its national language, what country's national flag has three horizontal strips of 'rojo, amarillo, rojo'; or 'vermell, groc, vermell', in its second language? This country has 19 'autonomies' (similar to the UK's counties, but much bigger). If you want to learn foreign national anthems, this is a good country to start with, as 'Marcha Real' has no words.

3

Called 'xióng māo' in Chinese Mandarin, what animals were the mascots used for the 2008 Summer Olympics in Beijing? The animal was represented in five different cartoon versions, which were called 'good luck dolls' or 'Fúwá'. If you've been constructively procrastinating on the Internet when doing maths homework you'll be aware of an amusing YouTube clip of a sneezing baby of this animal.

•

COMPUTING

1

Popularised by educational consultant Marc Prensky in a 2001 article, what two-word term is used to describe someone who grew up in the information or computer age? This would apply to children that could not imagine a world without chasing the streets for Pokémon GO, expecting to order an Amazon delivery in the morning and receive it by the evening, or streaming a Netflix movie within seconds. This term is in contrast to a 'Digital Immigrant'.

2

What is the word used to describe the process of removing defects or problems within a computer program, which prevent the smooth operation of the computer's system? Whilst it may sound like removing unwanted nits from your hair, this technique actually allows computer programmers to correct their mistakes.

3

What five-letter word is the smallest element of programmable colour on a computer display, such as an LCD screen? These elements are combined to form a complete image, video or anything visible on a computer display: from a noughts and crosses screenshot to a photo of a seagull in flight beside a monk in meditation... In digital imaging, this word is also known as 'dots' and may be the shortened form of the phrase 'picture element'.

•

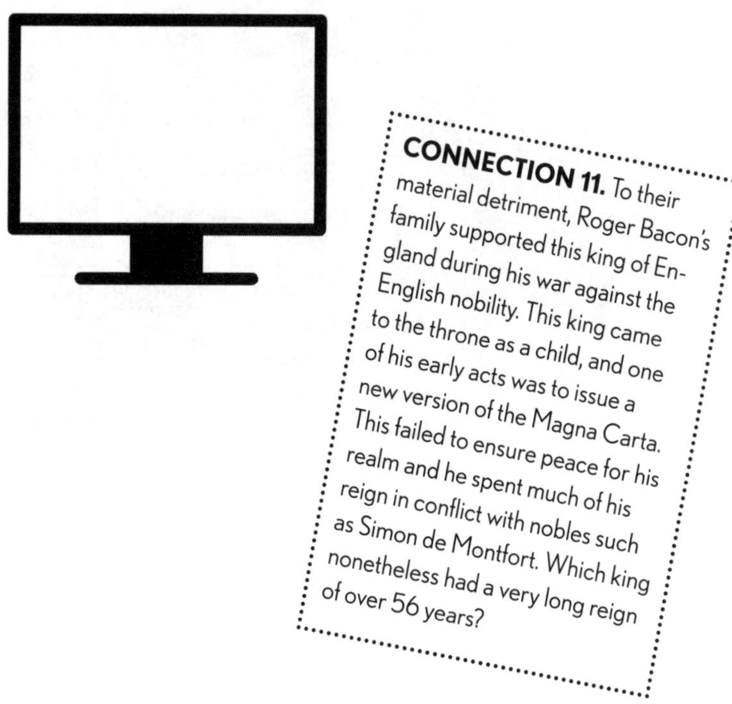

ANSWER 11 *Henry III* - ***Roger Bacon's family supported Henry III against the barons.***

CHRISTMAS

Eric and Bobby like to think that some readers might have received this quiz book as a Christmas gift. In which case, we hope you get to try this section of festive questions whilst stuffed like turkeys with roast potatoes and Brussels sprouts, sipping warm mulled wine and humming along to Mariah Carey. Bobby has to admit that if you ever play Mariah Carey's 'All I Want For Christmas Is You', you'll get him jumping about for joy and singing (terribly). Even if you play the song in summer.

CONNECTION 12. The three kings who followed Henry III all shared this name. The first king of England of this name built Harlech Castle as part of his campaign against Wales. The second king of this name lost the Battle of Bannockburn against Robert the Bruce. The third king of this name claimed the throne of France and instituted the Order of the Garter. What name is based on Old English words for 'rich' and 'guard'?

CHAPTER 28: 20 ALL I WANT FOR CHRISTMAS IS... CHRISTMAS-THEMED QUIZ QUESTIONS

1

In the classic Christmas novella by Charles Dickens, *A Christmas Carol*, what was the surname of Ebenezer Scrooge's deceased business partner? His surname is shared by a musician whose group was known as The Wailers, and the name of the titular dog in a 2008 American comedy-drama starring Owen Wilson and Jennifer Aniston.

2

The Christmas tree in London's Trafalgar Square has been donated by the inhabitants of which city each

ANSWER 12 *Edward (the kings are Edward I, Edward II and Edward III)* - **The three kings of England following Henry III were named Edward, a line ending with Edward III.**

year since 1947? This Scandinavian capital city is the home of the pop band A-ha, most renowned for their 1984 song 'Take On Me', and is where one of the versions of the famous Edvard Munch painting *The Scream* resides. *The Scream*: an accurate representation of the way many people feel during the lead-up to Christmas.

3

What connects 'I Want to Hold Your Hand' by The Beatles in 1963, 'Bohemian Rhapsody' by Queen in 1975, 'Don't You Want Me' by The Human League in 1981, 'Always on My Mind' by the Pet Shop Boys in 1987, 'Can We Fix It? by Bob the Builder in 2000 and most recently 'Rockabye' by Clean Bandit (featuring Sean Paul and Anne-Marie) in 2016?

4

What is the significance of Melchior, Caspar and Balthazar in the Christmas Nativity Story? The answer is also part of the name of a song released by James Blunt in his 2004 album

Back to Bedlam, and of a cocktail which blends three types of whisky (Scotch, Tennessee and Kentucky) together.

5

It may help if you listen to the different versions of the Band Aid charity song 'Do They Know It's Christmas' for this. What links Paul Young from the 1984 version, Kylie Minogue from the 1989 version, Chris Martin from the 2004 version and One Direction from the 2014 version?

6

The tradition of the Royal Christmas Message first started with a radio broadcast by King George V on the BBC's Empire Service. What year in the 1930s was this? This year also saw the 10th Summer Olympics in Los Angeles, the discovery of the neutron by English physicist Sir James Chadwick, the opening of the infamous Ashes cricket 'bodyline' series and, most importantly, the production of the first Mars Bar in England.

7

Refer to the carol, 'The Twelve Days of Christmas' to help with this mental maths gymnastics. Multiply the number of Calling Birds by the number of Drummers Drumming. Add this to the number of Turtle Doves. With this sum, divide it by the number of Lords a-Leaping. The total number you end up with gives which gift on that number's day, according to the song?

8

If you had a list of eight of Santa's reindeer from the 1823 poem 'A Visit From St Nicholas' (commonly called 'The Night Before Christmas') which letter of the alphabet would be the most common initial letter from all their names?

9

Though Christmas is not a national holiday in Japan, what global fast-food do an estimated 3.6 million families treat themselves to on

CONNECTION 13. Edward III contributed £16 towards the ransom of this man, who had been captured by the French during the Hundred Years' War. He worked as a civil servant as well as a soldier, but he is better known for other endeavours. He wrote *The Parlement of Foules* – which was written in reference to singing birds; not a commentary on politicians. Who also wrote a set of stories connected by a frame narrative about a group of travellers?

25th December? This chain ran a marketing campaign in 1974 to promote this, called 'Kurisumasu ni wa Kentakkii', which proved so popular that customers now sometimes have to place Christmas orders two months in advance.

10

You'll need to use your extensive knowledge of 2013 smash-hit Disney film *Frozen* for this question. Take the first letters of the following answers to give you a popular Christmas food:

A) What type of weather didn't seem to bother the Snow Queen?

B) The eighteen-year old younger sister, Princess of Arendelle.

C) The iceman who is accompanied by Sven the reindeer.

D) The twenty-one year old elder sister, Snow Queen of Arendelle.

11

Canadian postal codes have six characters, alternating letters and numbers (e.g. J4P 3B6). What is the Canadian postcode for Santa Claus?

ANSWER 13 *Geoffrey Chaucer* - ***Edward III helped pay a ransom for Chaucer when he was captured during the Hundred Years' War.***

12

Händel's oratorio *The Messiah* is often performed around Christmastime (Eric enjoys regularly attending a Toronto singalong). Its original performance in 1742 took place in April, however, and proceeds from the first performance were used to free 142 people from debtors' prison. In what city did *The Messiah* première?

13

A painting by Emanuel Leutze depicts this event. The painting in turn was featured on an American quarter commemorating New Jersey, where the event took place. This event was followed by a battle between the Continental Army and Hessian soldiers. What event took place on Christmas Day, 1776?

14

In 2018, Eastern Orthodox Christmas takes place on January 7. Isaac Newton was born on Christmas Day, January 4, 1643. Under what calendar, established by a military leader who gave his name to a month, do these two dates fall on December 25th?

15

Christmas Island, Norfolk Island, the Cocos (Keeling) Islands and an Antarctic territory are all external territories of which sovereign state?

16

According to a (probably legendary) story, St Nicholas punched Arius because of a theological dispute that arose during this event. This event was arranged by the Roman Emperor Constantine the Great in order to resolve the dispute in question. What council of bishops held in 325 AD gives its name to a Christian Creed?

17

This June 1645 battle was fought between Royalists led by Charles I and Prince Rupert, and Parliamentarians led by Sir Thomas Fairfax and Oliver Cromwell. King Charles lost the battle, which result would prove decisive to the outcome of the English Civil War. According to the song 'The World Turned Upside Down', at what battle was Christmas killed, referring to the Parliamentarians' opposition to its observance?

18

Wenceslaus Square, where a statue of the Good King (actually a duke) stands, is located in which central European capital city?

19

In O. Henry's short story 'The Gift of the Magi', husband and wife Jim and Della surprise each other with Christmas gifts. Della sold her hair so she could afford to get Jim a watch chain for his heirloom watch. What did Jim buy for Della with the money he got for selling his watch?

20

Multiply the number of lights on a Hanukkah menorah by the number of ships that came sailing in. Subtract the number of gospels that mention Jesus's earthly birth. What is the resulting number?

•

THE FINAL CHALLENGE

Ah, the Tossup round to end it all. Like the Starter for 10s but more quick-fire, in this round, if your team answers correctly, you get the chance to win points by answering the three bonus questions directly following. By now, you should be used to the question-and-answer format: this round is going to be fast, furious and final. May the best team win.

CONNECTION 14. This poet was buried near Chaucer in Westminster Abbey. His memorial describes him as 'THE PRINCE OF POETS IN HIS TYME'. He was a contemporary of Shakespeare, so this description is arguably a bit of an exaggeration. Who was awarded a pension by Elizabeth I, a person allegorically represented in his poetry?

CHAPTER 29: 40 BUZZER-STYLE TRIVIA TOSSUPS (10 SETS OF 4 QUESTIONS)

TOSSUP 1

A principle named for this man roughly states that humanity is not special. A transuranic element was named in honour of this man because he 'changed our view of the world.' This man also appears on a now-withdrawn banknote with a face value of 1,000 złoty. What 15th and 16th-century astronomer provided an early description of what is known today as Gresham's law, alongside other trifling contributions?

Bonuses 1: Japanese Politicians

1

This man was Prime Minister of Japan from 2006 to 2007, and became Prime Minister again in 2012. His name has been combined with the word 'economics' to form a portmanteau used to describe some of his policies. Who is he?

ANSWER 14
Edmund Spenser - ***Chaucer is buried near Edmund Spenser***.

2

This man, a graduate of University College London, is considered to be the first Prime Minister of Japan. He subsequently served as Japanese Resident-General in Korea. He was assassinated in 1909 by Ahn Jung-geun, a Korean nationalist. Who is this prime minister?

3

This woman became Governor of Tokyo in 2016. A member of the Liberal Democratic Party until 2017, she previously served as environment minister and then as defence minister in the Cabinet of Japan. Who is this woman?

TOSSUP 2

The giant rafflesia flower and the gingko biloba tree are examples of plants with this official classification. Both appear on the International Union for Conservation of

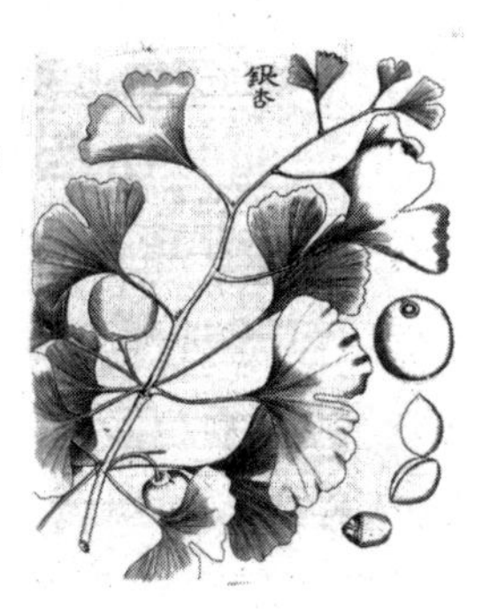

Nature's 'Red List', a compilation of organisms with this classification. The CITES treaty regulates international trade in organisms with this classification. What term is used to refer to organisms at risk of extinction, including the whooping crane and the blue whale?

Bonuses 2: Geographic Homophones

1

One is a city, the place where Sir Alexander Burnes was killed and the location of the Bala Hissar fort. The other is a term for a group of plotters or an acronym referring to several advisors of Charles II. What words are these?

2

One is a federal city which gives its name to an international agreement governing copyright. The other is an injury that is divided into degrees denoting severity. What words are these?

3

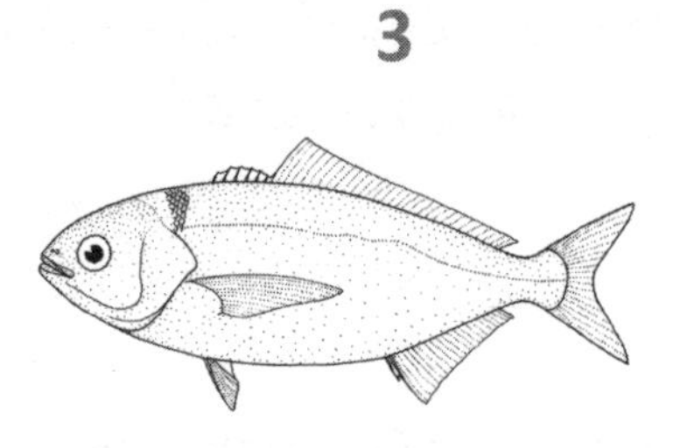

One is a city on the Han river, the location of the 1988 Summer Olympics. The other can be used to refer to several species of flatfish, including a striped one with the scientific name *Aesopia cornuta*. What words are these?

TOSSUP 3

One of this artist's paintings features two men, submerged in mud and soil up to their knees. Instead of helping each other out, the two men are hitting each other with sticks. This artist is also famous for making two paintings of the same woman to suit different levels of prudishness. What Spanish artist

CONNECTION 15. Critics have noted similarities between one of this author's major works and Spenser's *The Faerie Queene*. This author met Galileo Galilei in Florence, and was impressed by this 'Tuscan Artist' with an 'Optic Glass' who looked for new features on the moon. Meeting this house-arrested enemy of the church left a deep impression on the author, who later supported freedom of the press in his *Areopagitica*. What author served as Secretary for Foreign Tongues during the Commonwealth period?

painted the family of Charles IV, as well as paintings depicting the Napoleonic wars in Spain?

Bonuses 3: Economic Laws

1

This economic 'law' basically states that 'the bad drives out the good'. Generally speaking, if coins of lesser intrinsic value are declared to be of equal monetary value to coins of greater intrinsic value, the coins of greater value will be withdrawn from circulation. What law is named for an advisor to Elizabeth I?

2

Paul Krugman referred to this theory to explain why a country does not need a more competitive economy than its trading partners to benefit from international trade. What theory was illustrated with reference to production of wine and cloth in Portugal and the United Kingdom?

ANSWER 15
John Milton - ***John Milton referred to Edmund Spenser as greater than Aquinas.***

3

This theory was discussed by scholars of the School of Salamanca and by Jean Bodin. The theory basically states that prices will rise if the amount of money in an economy increases without a corresponding increase in the amount of goods, and prices will fall if the amount of money decreases without a corresponding decrease in the amount of goods. What theory is being described?

TOSSUP 4

The XV International Brigade, a force fighting on the side of the Spanish Republic in the Spanish Civil War, was nicknamed after which historical figure? He allegedly grew his iconic beard after a young lady wrote to him, saying 'All the ladies like whiskers'. His son served as United States Secretary of War under James Garfield and Chester Arthur, who sound like a pair of cats. Suetonius is the name of Eyewear Publishing's cat-editor!

Bonuses 4: Gilbert and Sullivan

1

A character in Gilbert and Sullivan's *Utopia, Limited* states that he is in communication with the title character of this operetta, whom he describes as 'a leading authority' on punishment. One character in this operetta claims to be an archbishop, attorney general and Lord High Auditor – a rather incongruous selection of professions, given the setting of the show. Which operetta is described here?

2

This operetta opened in 1882, in the same year that the 'Brush Boom' occurred, a speculative frenzy over electricity companies listed in London. A character in this operetta sings about a dream he had that involves stock market speculation around a scheme to plant tradespeople in the ground, so that they literally grow their wares. Which operetta is described here?

3

This operetta premiered in New York in 1879. A character in this operetta promises to do something in 1940, when he will finally be freed from an indenture. A different character refers to Gilbert and Sullivan's previous operetta HMS Pinafore as an 'infernal nonsense', even though he claims he can 'whistle all the airs from' said piece. Gilbert and Sullivan: heralds of postmodernism. Which operetta is described here?

TOSSUP 5

This woman briefly mistook a close friend for a gardener. Upon recognising him, she rushed to share news of him with his other friends, leading Catholics to refer to her as 'Apostle of the Apostles'. According to the Gospel of Luke, from what woman did 'seven devils' come out?

Bonuses 5: Native American, Mesoamerican and South American Leaders

1

This man claimed his throne by overthrowing his brother Huáscar in a civil war. He would later be captured by Francisco Pizarro at Cajamarca in what is now Peru. Which Sapa Inca is depicted in a dramatic historical painting by John Everett Millais, the saccharine Pre-Raphaelite painter of children, cherries and bubbles?

2

This Shawnee leader fought on the British side during the War of 1812. Prior to that war, he fought against the Americans at the Battle of Tippecanoe. Alongside Isaac Brock, he helped to capture Fort Detroit, and he was later killed at the Battle of the Thames. He was admired by the father of one William Sherman, who gave said William this Native American's name as a middle name. Ironically, William Sherman became a general in the Union army during the US Civil War, and an American hero.

3

The 'Halls' of this leader are mentioned in the American 'Marines' Hymn'. However, they really should have fact-checked their lyrics, as they refer to the Battle of Chapultepec, which occurred over three centuries after this leader's death, at a castle which was only begun in 1785. Which Aztec leader built a new palace in Tenochtitlan and was later taken prisoner by the Spanish?

•

CONNECTION 16. This philosopher refers to Milton's descriptions of Satan as an example of 'the sublime', a concept he largely defined. As a member of parliament, this man was famously dramatic, and led the prosecution trial at the impeachment of Warren Hastings with a speech including the line 'I impeach him in the name of human nature itself, which he has cruelly outraged, injured and oppressed'. If only the Prime Minister's Questions were as polite and restrained today. Who is considered to be one of the founders of the modern conservative tradition, and was credited by Carlyle as one of the first people to refer to the press as the 'fourth estate'?

TOSSUP 6

A test with this code name occurred near a desert called the 'Journada del Meurto', or the 'Journey of Death'. Isidor Isaac Rabi described the result of the test as 'a vision which was seen with more than the eye'. Robert Oppenheimer claimed to have recalled the words 'Now I am become death, the destroyer of worlds' from the *Bhagavad-Gita* after witnessing the results of the test. Rather less pretentiously, a physicist named Kenneth Bainbridge may have spoken the words: 'We're all sons of bitches now.'

Bonuses 6: Events and People Depicted in Art

1

These men were depicted in a painting by Benjamin West for George III. They were also depicted in a sculpture by Rodin, the original of which is located in a city in Northern France and a copy of which is located near the British Parlia-

ANSWER 16
Edmund Burke - ***Burke praised Milton as 'sublime'.***

ment buildings. Which six men, according to Jean Froissart, offered their lives to Edward III to end a siege, and were spared at the behest of his wife Queen Phillipa?

2

This event may sound French in character, but in fact is nothing of the kind. It is depicted in several paintings by Peter Paul Rubens, one notable example of which is located in the National Gallery, London and one of which is in the Prado, Madrid. The event has also been depicted by Lucas Cranach the Elder. Which event revolved around a simple decision: to which one of three ladies to give a particular fruit?

3

A fresco by Cesare Maccari depicting this event is located in the Palazzo Madama in Rome. The Italian Senate meets in the Palazzo, so the subject of the painting is appropriate. In the painting, a different Senate is shown listening to a man in a toga. The painting includes many empty seats surrounding one individual, the subject of the speech. (Perhaps he was overly fond of Italian cologne.) What event is shown?

TOSSUP 7

This man was created a Knight of the Thistle, one of Scotland's highest honours. However, this man was born and lived very far from Scotland. When he wasn't called 'Sir Robert', he was sometimes called 'Pig Iron Bob' or 'Ming'. What man served as Prime Minister of Australia from 1939 to 1941 and from 1949 to 1966?

Bonuses 7: Australasian Wildlife

1

Species belonging to this family of birds are found in New Guinea, Indonesia and Australia. According to Jared Diamond, some species belonging to this family of birds may transmit patterns for nests culturally. What family of birds is known for the elaborate nests which males build to attract females?

2

The two species of this reptile are the only remaining members of the order *Rhynchocephalia*. The common name used for these species comes from Maori and describes the scaly spine on their backs. What species, noted for their 'third eye' are found in parts of New Zealand?

3

This mammal species is notable for a contagious cancer, spread by biting. Now rare, they were once considered a nuisance, and in the 1800s, the Van Dieman's Land Company put a bounty on their furry little heads to encourage

CONNECTION 17. This man described Edmund Burke as a sycophant for hire, willing to support the American Revolution for pecuniary gain and oppose the French one for similar reasons. This man believed in the labour theory of value, whereby the value of a good is determined by the amount of work put in to make it. What man had a city named after him from 1953 to 1990, though it is now known as Chemnitz?

hunting of these animals. What ferocious, carnivorous, marsupial mammal is native to an Australian state?

TOSSUP 8

Al-Qarawiyyin, in Fez, Morocco, is perhaps the oldest of these institutions in the world. The honourable Al-Azhar in Cairo is a younger example, but still pretty venerable, at over 1,000 years old. Bologna, Italy has one of these institutions, as does Salamanca, Spain. Sites of youth and age: what type of institution is referred to here?

Bonuses 8: Latin Terms

1

A modified version of this three-word saying was allegedly sent to Pope Innocent XI by Polish King Jan III Sobieski following the Siege of Vienna. His new, slightly less egomaniacal, version gave credit to God for victory. What pompous saying, in its original form, is associated with the Battle of Zela?

ANSWER 17

Karl Marx - ***Marx described Burke as a sycophant for hire.***

2

'*Timeo Danaos et dona ferentes*' is, unsurprisingly, written in Latin, not in Greek. The phrase comes from Virgil's *Aeneid*, where it is delivered by Laocoön. What is the English translation of the phrase given as a warning to the people of Troy after they received their eponymous horse? The original is not quite colloquial – a rough translation is also accepted.

3

In Stephen Leacock's short story 'Lord Oxhead's Secret', Lord Oxhead's family motto is '*Hic, haec, hoc, hujus, hujus, hujus*'. This motto is actually several declensions of a word. What is that word's translation(s) in English?

TOSSUP 9

Like another melancholy Dane, this author spent time in Elsinore (he attended school there). He wrote a tale about a 'Great Sea-Serpent' that turns out to be the trans-Atlantic telegraph cable. What author is known for stories including 'The Princess and the Pea', 'The Brave Tin Soldier' and 'The Little Mermaid'?

Bonuses 9: Presidents of the Royal Society of London

1

This surgeon invented a machine that sprays carbolic acid; for what possible use seems impossible to imagine. In fact, it was of great benefit to medical science: he was inspired by Louis Pasteur's theory of small entities called 'germs', to introduce antiseptic methods into surgery, in which germs would be killed by carbolic acid. As a surgeon, he also later pioneered aseptic surgery, in which sterilisation methods are used to exclude germs in the first place. Which surgeon is referred to here?

2

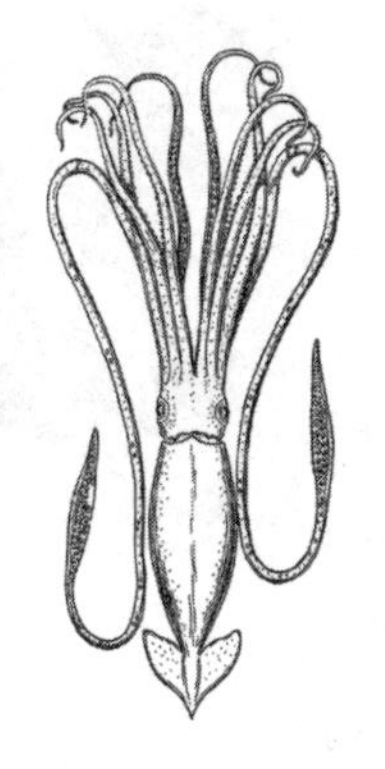

One man with this surname performed experiments on squid nerve cells. His grandfather, with the same surname, was nicknamed 'Darwin's bulldog', and was mocked for supporting the theory that man is related to monkeys. Keeping it in the family, what is the surname of this grand-father and grandson who both served as Presidents of the Royal Society?

3

This man had many roles. He served as a Member of Parliament, Master of the Mint and Lucasian Professor of Mathematics at Cambridge University. What man wrote *The Chronology of Ancient Kingdoms Amended,* as well as other more notable works?

CONNECTION 18. The zoologist Ray Lankester attended Karl Marx's funeral. Ray Lankester is mentioned in this author's 1912 novel *Marriage*. This author, an advocate of free love, is most famous for his science fiction novels, including books about a time traveller and one involving a Martian invasion of Earth. What author's name could also be a place where one could find mercury?

TOSSUP 10

This mathematician was influenced by the works of al-Khwarizmi. He shares his real name with another famous Italian, but he is commonly known by a different name, applied to him after his death. What Italian mathematician from Pisa is famous for a sequence of numbers that he used to determine the dizzying rate of growth of a population of rabbits?

Bonuses 10: Add a 'G'

1

One word means a rivulet. Add a 'g' to the beginning of this word to get a second word, the implement that led to St Lawrence's demise. (HINT: he was not eaten after his death, though the manner of his death might suggest it.) What are the two words?

ANSWER 18 *Herbert George Wells (or HG Wells; the chemical symbol for mercury is Hg)* – ***Marx's funeral was attended by Ray Lankester. Ray Lankester was an inspiration for a character in a work by H.G. Wells.***

2

One word is the name of an Italian city famous for cloth (well, one individual cloth, at least). Add a 'g' to the end of this word to get a second word, the name of a mathematician whose name appears alongside that of Alonzo Church in a hypothesis regarding computable functions. What are the two words?

3

One word is the surname of a banking family that included a Governor of the Bank of England (the Earl of Cromer). Add a 'g' to the middle of this name to get a present participle for 'bursting in' or a gerund for the movement of goods by a type of canal boat.

•

CONNECTION 19. Hilaire Belloc criticised HG Wells for devoting more space in his *Outline of History* to the Persian wars than to the life of which man?

ANSWER 19 *Jesus Christ.*

ANSWERS!

STARTERS

CHAPTER 1: 30 STARTER FOR 10s

1 *Arthur C. Clarke.*

2 *Four.*

3 *William Gladstone. He was known by the acronym 'GOM' by his fans, standing for 'Grand Old Man' – though Queen Victoria is likely to have agreed with some detractors who claimed that it stood for 'God's Only Mistake'.*

4 *The beheading of St John the Baptist.*

5 *The okapi (*Okapia johnstoni*).*

6 *Maryam Mirzakhani.*

7 *Brazzaville and Kinshasa.*

8 *E-S-C-H-E-R-I-C-H-I-A. If you spelt it correctly, chances are you pronounced it incorrectly. There are no diseases including the letters 'B-O-B-B-Y'.*

9 *Technetium.*

10 *Amnesty International.*

11 *Retained the Champions League (or won consecutive championships).*

12 *Parrot (*Flaubert's Parrot *is the Barnes novel).*

13 *The Lloyd's building.*

14 Henry V.

15 *The* Symphonie Fantastique.

16 *Elinor Ostrom.*

17 *Fabergé (House of Fabergé).*

18 *King James I of England (James VI of Scotland).*

19 *Grit.*

20 *Daniel Day-Lewis (his father was Cecil Day-Lewis). Playing Hamlet in 1989, Daniel was so overcome with empathy during the scene where Hamlet's father's ghost appears that he began* *sobbing with filial grief, and could not continue in the play.*

21 *Kerala.*

22 *Dennis Gabor. Inventor of the epitome of celebrity, Zsa Zsa Gabor?*

23 *Seven.*

24 *Nadine Gordimer.*

25 *James, with six (Madison, Monroe, Polk, Buchanan, Garfield and 'Jimmy' Carter). William and John are tied second with four instances each.*

26 *1510s (1511, 1519, 1519, 1517).*

27 *Ear ('Anvil Chorus', 'Hammer of the Scots', stirrup).*

28 *Suspension of disbelief.*

29 *Shirley Temple.*

30 *Pelé.*

CHAPTER 2: 60 BONUS QUESTIONS (20 SETS OF 3)

1a *1916.*

1b *Leonid Brezhnev.*

1c *King Edward VII (in 1908).*

2a *Florence Nightingale.*

2b *George Stephenson.*

2c *Sir John Houblon.*

3a *Carol Dweck.*

3b How to Win Friends and Influence People.

3c *Malcolm Gladwell.*

4a *Hannah Fry.*

4b *Rachel Riley.*

4c *Simon Singh. Interestingly, Simon's elder brother, Tom Singh, is the founder of the UK's* New Look *chain of fashion stores. A talented family indeed.*

5a *Bertram 'Bertie' Wooster.*

5b *Captain Hook in JM Barrie's* Peter Pan.

5c *James Bond.*

6a *Lehman Brothers.*

6b *Goldman Sachs.*

6c *HSBC (Originally Hongkong and Shanghai Banking Corporation).*

7a *UCL (University College London).*

7b *Edinburgh.*

7c *Royal Holloway.*

8a *Julian of Norwich.*

8b *St Francis of Assisi.*

8c *St Bonaventure.*

9a *Captain Flint.*

9b *Jonathan Livingston Seagull.*

9c *Iago.*

10a *1895.*

10b *Martin Peters.*

10c *Boleyn Ground.*

11a *Joe Wicks.*

11b *Shaun T.*

11c *Mr Motivator (or Derrick Evans).*

12a *Riz Ahmed. You can see* The One Show *clip here! https://youtu.be/bkwp6P6W7Ew*

12b *Rushanara Ali.*

12c *Konnie Huq.*

13a *Enfield.*

13b *Newham.*

13c *Merton.*

14a *Björk (Guðmundsdóttir).*

14b *Sigrid (Solbakk Raabe).*

14c *ABBA.*

15a *Russell Group.*

15b *RA Butler (Rab Butler).*

15c *Ofsted (Office for Standards in Education, Children's Services and Skills).*

16a *Nihonium.*

16b *Moscovium.*

16c *Tennessine.*

17a *Michael Morpurgo.*

17b *Jacqueline Wilson.*

17c *Malorie Blackman.*

18a *Jeff Bezos.*

18b *Jack Ma.*

18c *Pierre Omidyar.*

19a *Sir Richard Owen.*

19b Nature.

19c *Iridium.*

20a *Muse.*

20b *Paganini.*

20c Shine.

CATEGORIES

SPORTS

CHAPTER 3: 10 WORDS IN THE NAMES OF BRITISH FOOTBALL CLUBS

1 *Arsenal.*

2 *United (the Middle Eastern nation is the United Arab Emirates, the sovereign state off the northern coast of Europe is the United Kingdom and the country in North America is the United States of America).*

3 *Villa.*

4 *Wanderer.*

5 *Albion.*

6 *New Saints.*

7 *Rangers.*
8 *The Crystal Palace.*
9 *Sir Henry Percy (nicknamed Harry Hotspur).*
10 *Wednesday.*

CHAPTER 4: 20 SPORTS TIME!

1 *Beijing (its motto being 'A pure passion for ice and snow' – Princess Elsa from Disney's* Frozen *would have loved this).*
2 Invictus.
3 *The Boat Race between Oxford and Cambridge universities. Though there is arguably even more tension when a Cambridge college takes on an Oxford college on* University Challenge.
4 *Nike (though it wouldn't have counted as a world record, as it was not done in race conditions). To imagine how fast this is, try running 100m in 17 seconds. Then do this another 421 times at 17 seconds each!*
5 *Freddie Mercury. Bobby's father bought him a sports almanac for the Barcelona games in 1992 and this is what sparked his love for sport. (And, indeed, numbers; Bobby studiously wrote down the results and timings of every single event!)*
6 *Dame Ellen MacArthur, from Derbyshire. Interestingly, she has released several ecological economic reports about reconfiguring the economy from linear (wasteful) to circular (waste-free).*
7 Escape to Victory *(or,* Victory *in North America).*
8 *John Landy.*
9 *Canada vs. United States at St George's Cricket Club in New York. And yet, Eric can attest*

that cricket doesn't quite hold the same sway in his native Canadian homeland as it does for Bobby's parents' homeland of India.

10 *Phelps raced a great white shark as part of Discovery Channel's* Shark Week. *The man managed 38.1 seconds but the CGI monster won by two seconds. Insurance companies probably didn't want to risk a celebrity being eaten on live TV.*

11 *Marilyn Monroe (she was also married to Arthur Miller from 1956-61, one of the finest playwrights of the 20th century, as many GCSE English Literature students will know from studying* Death of a Salesman *and* The Crucible*).*

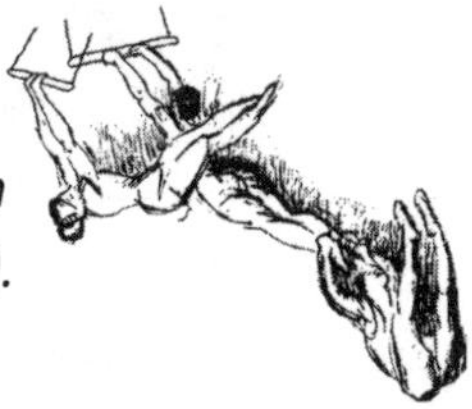

12 *Sue Barker.*

13 *A perfect 10 in gymnastics (in the uneven bars for Nadia, the scoreboard said 1.00).*

14 *Bobby Fischer.*

15 *Albatross (condor is the unofficial term for four under par and has never been achieved in a professional tournament). Bobby is pushing for a 'seagull' to become a term in golf as well.*

16 *Henry Russell Sanders (no relation to KFC's Colonel Sanders).*

17 *Reddit (founded by Ohanian and roommate Steven Huffman at the University of Virginia).*

18 *Respectively, Carl Lewis and the world record holder Mike Powell. Lewis had been undefeated in the long jump for a decade, winning 65 consecutive events until that day in Tokyo.*

19 *Eton College. Bobby played the Field Game when at Eton's Sixth Form, and it took him a while to understand the rules of this rugby/football-*

based game! At his East London state school, Bobby used to play a version of Eton Fives called slap-ball with a tennis ball and the back of staff room walls.

20 *Aamir Khan the actor (and Amir Khan the boxer). Bobby watched the film in a cinema in Delhi on holiday and can attest it has true Disney feel-good qualities as well as a motivational soundtrack to which Bobby writes quiz questions.*

ARTS AND HUMANITIES

CHAPTER 5: 10 RED, YELLOW AND BLUE – THE ARTS

1 *They are names of the Teenage Mutant Ninja Turtles. The art works are by Donatello, Michelangelo, Leonardo (da Vinci) and Raphael.*

2 *The Golden Gate Bridge.*

3 Sgt. Pepper's Lonely Hearts Club Band *by The Beatles.*

4 *Quentin Blake. Quentin was a childhood family friend of Bobby. Bobby and his elder brother Davey bombarded the artist with hundreds of drawings they copied from Roald Dahl books. Bobby's father was persuaded to spend significant amounts at the Post Office when sending these, in a large parcel, by registered post. Quentin was so bowled over that he sent personalised drawings and handmade birthday cards to the boys.*

5 *Alberto Korda, using a Leica M2 camera loaded with Kodak Plus-X pan film. Yes, people used to use actual cameras rather than mobile phones to take photos.*

6 *Johannes Vermeer. There is still currently a $10m reward for information on these thefts. D'oh.*

7 *The Terracotta Army – believe it or not, each warrior is unique, no two faces are alike.*

8 *Sir Christopher Wren (most famous for St Paul's Cathedral, of course. Paul shouldn't get all the credit.)*

9 *The ArcelorMittal Orbit (for those with strong stomachs, the structure now has the world's tallest and longest tunnel slide at 178m).*

10 *The Turbine Hall (the works described are Salcedo's* Shibboleth, *Ai Weiwei's* Sunflower Seeds, *Rachel Whiteread's* EMBANKMENT *and Olafur Eliasson's* The Weather Project.

CHAPTER 6: 10 LITERATURE

1 *Stephen Leacock.*

2 *HP Lovecraft.*

3 The Frogs *(Gilbert and Sullivan's Modern Major General claims to know the 'croaking chorus' in this play).*

4 Le Rouge et le Noir *(or* The Red and the Black; *or* The Scarlet and the Black*).*

5 Kim.

6 *Don Juan/Don Giovanni.*

7 *Rabindranath Tagore.*

8 The Travels of Marco Polo (*or* The Book of the Marvels of the World, The Description of the World, Il Milione).

9 *Edgar Allan Poe. The works referred to are 'The Pit and the Pendulum', 'The Cask of Amontillado', 'The Raven' (the bird) and 'The Gold-Bug' (the bug).*

10 *Winston Churchill (the author of the book about the revolution was Winston Spencer Churchill, later Prime Minister of the United Kingdom).*

CHAPTER 7: 10 ENGLISH WORDS OF NON-INDO-EUROPEAN ORIGIN

1 *Guano.*

2 *Shaman.*

3 *Mamba (*Dendroapsis *translates to 'tree asp').*

4 *Caucus.*

5 *The quetzal (a good word for Scrabble).*

6 *The sauna.*

7 *To kowtow.*

8 *Amok/amuck.*

9 *Mana.*

10 *'Chrys-' (chrysanthemum, John Chrysostom [the 'golden-mouthed'] and chrysalis).*

CHAPTER 8: 10 NAMES OF BOOKS IN THE OLD TESTAMENT OF THE BIBLE

1 *Genesis (the inflatable space modules are Genesis I and Genesis II).*

2 *Judges.*

3 *Daniel.*

4 *Ruth (Element 104 is Rutherfordium, element 44 is Ruthenium, 'the Bambino' is Babe Ruth and the Associate Justice is Ruth Bader Ginsburg).*

5 *Numbers (Ramanujan's number is 1729. Upon hearing that his friend arrived in a taxicab with that number, Ramanujan remarked that 1729 is the smallest number that can be written as the sum of two different cubes, namely $1^3 + 12^3$ and $9^3 + 10^3$).*

6 *Exodus.*

7 *Kings (Jean-Baptiste Bernadotte became King Charles XIV & III John of Sweden and Norway; The Shakespeare quotes are from* Richard II*).*

8 *Psalms ('Va, pensiero' is inspired by Psalm 137).*

9 *Ecclesiastes (Ecclesiasticus is the book in the apocrypha).*

10 *Lamentations (though some are Laments).*

CHAPTER 9: 11 WORDS THAT ARE ASSOCIATED WITH COLOURS

1 *Rubric.*

2 *Oolong tea (the name comes from* 乌龙*, or Wūlóng in Mandarin).*

3 *Colorado.*

4 *Lapis lazuli. The southern coast of France is the Côte d'Azur. 'Azur' and the English word 'Azure' comes from 'lazuli'. The word 'lazuli' comes from Lajward, a place in the Badakhshan region of Central Asia. It's like a 'change one letter' puzzle, played over hundreds of years.*

5 *Bears. The Russian word for bear is 'medved', which roughly means 'the honey-loving one'. Polar bears are generally carnivorous, while panda bears are generally herbivorous. 'Paddington' generally eats marmalade. His name, along with those of 'Rupert' and 'Teddy' might be a nickname, though probably not given out of fear in these cases.*

6 *Beluga (as in beluga caviar, beluga sturgeon and beluga whales).*

7 *White ('album' is used to refer to a blank*

white tablet in Latin; 'albumen' is the part of an egg that turns white when cooked).

8 *The Phoenicians ('phoinós' is Greek for 'blood red', perhaps a reference to the purple dyes produced and traded by the Phoenicians).*

9 Éminence grise*; or 'grey eminence' – eerie indeed. Note that Capuchin friars wear brown robes, so the name may not be a reference to the specific colour of Père Joseph's clothing.*

10 *The Byzantine Empire (or the Eastern Roman Empire).*

11 *Dublin, Ireland.*

MATHS AND SCIENCE

CHAPTER 10: 10 MATHS AND SCIENCE

1 *Taylor Series (Brook Taylor was a 17th- and 18th-century English mathematician).*

2 *Tide.*

3 *Neutrinos.*

4 *Entropy (the equation on Boltzmann's tomb is S = k log W, where S is a measure of entropy in a system, W is the number of possible microstates in which the system could be in, and k is Boltzmann's constant).*

5 *A white dwarf; neither white, small, nor humanoid.*

6 *Inflation.*

7 *RAM (or random-access memory).*

8 *A complex number. (A simple answer.)*

9 *Lava (magma is inside the earth, while lava is outside).*

10 *The Neanderthal.*

CHAPTER 11: 10 UNITS

1 *Smoot.*
2 *Bath.*
3 *Shake.*
4 *Li.*
5 *Buckingham.*
6 *Friedman (the columnist is Thomas Friedman, the gubernatorial candidate is Richard 'Kinky' Friedman and the economist is Milton Friedman).*
7 *Scruple.*
8 *International units.*
9 *Parsec.*
10 *Max Planck.*

CHAPTER 12: 10 EQUATIONS AND STATEMENTS

1 c (Boyle)
2 i (Bayes)
3 f (Hooke)
4 e (Pythagoras)
5 j (Heisenberg)
6 b (Fisher)
7 d (Newton)
8 h (Euler)
9 a (Einstein)
10 g (Fermat)

CHAPTER 13: 10 DISCREDITED THEORIES

1 *Mesmerism/Animal magnetism.*
2 *Tycho Brahe.*
3 *Lamarckian evolution.*
4 *The four humours (also accept blood, phlegm, black bile and yellow bile).*
5 *Piltdown man.*

6 *Alchemy (the Greek word is* khēmia, *from the Egyptian Kmt; Rutherford was able to change nitrogen into oxygen, achieving transmutation of an element, if not to gold; Glenn Seaborg turned bismuth into gold, but at prohibitive cost).*

7 *Phrenology or cranioscopy.*

8 *Luminiferous aether (or aether, or ether; not to be mistaken for the chemical with formula* $(C_2H_5)_2O$ *and related compounds).*

9 *The plum pudding model.*

10 *Steady-state theory.*

CHAPTER 14: 10 NO DIMINISHING RETURNS TO KNOWLEDGE! – BUSINESS, ECONOMICS AND FINANCE

1 *Milton Keynes (Milton Friedman and John Maynard Keynes).*

2 *Financial Times Stock Exchange. FTSE 100 are the top 100 companies listed on the London Stock Exchange. The term 'footsie' may also refer to a 'foot selfie'!*

3 *Lewis (Edward, Michael and Martin). Bobby is an ambassador alongside Martin Lewis for the charity National Numeracy which aims to improve numeracy in the country. Mr Seagull is a man on a numbers mission.*

4 *Tata (Tigger says 'ta-ta for now').*

5 *Hyperinflation. Whilst the image of children playing with stacks of hyperinflated currency like Lego bricks during the Weimar Republic are the most infamous images of this word, it was Hungary that suffered the worst case of hyperinflation. During one period, prices in*

Hungary doubled every 15 hours.

6 *Bank of England. Retiring as Secretary in 1908, he must have enjoyed escaping to the riverbank after what was clearly a stressful job.*

7 *Kentucky. Officially 'The Commonwealth of Kentucky', it is one of only four US states constituted as a commonwealth, alongside Virginia, Pennsylvania and Massachusetts.*

8 *Tang (AD 618-907).*

9 *Google (an accidental misspelling of 'googol').*

10 *These are the drinks drunk by UK Chancellors while making their annual Budget Speech to Parliament. By tradition, the Chancellor is allowed to drink anything, including alcohol, which is normally prohibited under parliamentary rules. Recent Chancellors such as Osborne, Darling and Brown have opted for the safe choice of water.*

HISTORY

CHAPTER 15: PARALLEL LIVES

1 *South Korea (the Republic of Korea) and Taiwan (the Republic of China).*

2 *Napoleon Bonaparte and Toyotomi Hideyoshi.*

3 *Mohandas Karamchand 'Mahatma' Gandhi and Nelson Mandela. Gandhi was referred to as 'bapu', 'father' in Gujarati. Mandela was referred to as 'tata', 'father' in Xhosa.*

4 *Boudicca and the Lakshmibai, the Rani of Jhansi.*

CHAPTER 16: 10 THE ROAD TO D-DAY

1 *The Dieppe Raid (or Operation Jubilee).*

2 *Trident.*

3 *Tanks.*
4 *Calais.*
5 *Double cross (twenty in Roman numerals is XX, a double cross).*
6 *Mulberry.*
7 *Dwight D. Eisenhower.*
8 *Erwin Rommel.*
9 *King George VI.*
10 *(Kingdom of) Italy. Usually nicknamed 'The Boot': something better designed for kicking underbellies.*

CHAPTER 17: 10 NATIONAL DAYS

1 *Canada (the Newfoundland Regiment fought in the Battle of the Somme near Beaumont Hamel, and suffered severe casualties).*
2 *Greenland.*
3 *Malta.*
4 *Portugal (Eric Monkman shares a birthday with Portugal Day).*
5 *The Falkland Islands.*
6 *Sweden (the king was Gustav Vasa).*
7 *Australia.*
8 *San Marino.*
9 *France – Bastille Day is the day's name in English, referring to the storming of the Bastille Prison in Paris that took place on July 14, 1789.*
10 *Taiwan, or the Republic of China (the day commemorates the Wuchang Uprising that took place in 1911, in what is now the People's Republic of China).*

CHAPTER 18: 10 BEFORE 1000 BC

1 *Hammurabi's Code (Shutruk-Nahunte once owned the finger-shaped stele on which Hammurabi's Code is inscribed. This copy is now in the Louvre).*
2 *Quadratic equations (or quadratical equations, in the song).*
3 *The Indus Valley Civilisation. They are also known as the Harappan Civilisation, a name that does not come from the name of a river, but is an acceptable answer.*
4 *Agamemnon (the Sophocles tragedy is* Electra*, the Gluck opera is* Iphigénie en Tauride*).*
5 *Diabetes.*
6 *Jericho.*
7 *The Shang Dynasty.*
8 *Ishtar (Akkadian)/Inanna (Sumerian).*
9 *The Hittites (they fought against Ramses II at Kadesh).*
10 *Akhenaten (or Amenhotep IV).*

MISCELLANEOUS KNOWLEDGE

CHAPTER 19: 20 THE PRICE OF A PINT OF MILK – POP CULTURE

1 *Formula One (motor racing).*
2 *Pokémon-GO.*
3 *Vermouth.*
4 Downton Abbey *(or 'Down-town Abbey', as Puff Daddy pronounces it in his spoof YouTube video, which features him as Lord Wolcott). Bobby is also a diehard 'Abbeyhead'.*
5 The Simpsons *(Mr Seagull the Maths teacher*

will have you know that the writers of The Simpsons *have embedded 'morsels of mathematics' into the minds of the viewers, according to Simon Singh's book about the show. Simon is an alumni of Emmanuel College too. Perhaps there is not such a gulf between 'price of milk' and conceptual philosophical theory).*

6 *Norah Jones (born Geetali Norah Shankar). After her parents separated in 1986, she adopted her mother's surname.*

7 *JK Rowling (a fourth novel,* Lethal White, *is in the pipeline). As a child, Rowling wanted to be called Ella Galbraith, apparently for no particular reason – and she is a fan of Robert F. Kennedy.*

8 *Edward Enninful.*

9 Bill & Ted's Excellent Adventure. *Easily confused with* Monkman & Seagull's Polymathic Adventure *which was also quite excellent, and, moreover, polymathic.*

10 Shark Tank.

11 *Saxe-Coburg-Gotha. A bit more of a mouthful than Windsor.*

12 The Book of Mormon.

13 *Boomerang.*

14 *Fidget spinners. Mr Seagull is not a fan of this addictive toy, which even manages to distract some of his students from his gripping explanations of Pythagoras' Theorem.*

15 *Australia. Makes total logical sense. Please, Santa, make Australia win and therefore be the hosts of Eurovision next year.*

16 University Challenge, *the annual Christmas*

version that comprises famous alumni. Did you think you could get through this book without a single answer being University Challenge*?*

17 *The Big Bang Theory. Fred Hoyle actually denies the term 'Big Bang' was pejorative as the image was meant to contrast with his preference of the alternate 'steady-state' cosmological model.*

18 *Georg Friedrich Händel and Jimi Hendrix. (Just imagine what a duo they would have been. Händel on the ivories, Jimi on the axe: watch those digits dance!)*

19 GQ. *Bobby was 'gassed' (colloquial for 'excited'), to be interviewed by them, previous Facebook Live interviewees having included boxer David Haye, actor Gerard Butler and sports presenter Gary Lineker.*

20 *These are sizes of wine bottles, though sadly the average person is unlikely to encounter any past Methuselah other than in a pub quiz.*

CHAPTER 20: 10 BEST PICTURE WINNERS OF THE PAST 10 YEARS (2006 TO 2016)

1 Moonlight.

2 *A spotlight.*

3 Twelve Years a Slave *(the film is* 12 Years a Slave*).*

4 Argo.

5 (The) Artist.

6 *King's speeches.*

7 The Hurt Locker.

8 Slumdog Millionaire. *Shah Rukh Khan turned down the opportunity to play the host of the Indian version of* Who Wants to be a Millionaire? *in the* *film. He was hosting the actual show at the time and he did not want people to think he would cheat like the host in the film.*

9 No Country For Old Men.

10 The Departed.

CHAPTER 21: 10 NON-CAPITAL CITIES

1 *Busan, South Korea, also known as Pusan.*

2 *Rio de Janeiro, Brazil.*

3 *Vitamin C, or ascorbic acid.*

4 *Kraków.*

5 *Marseilles, France. The French national anthem, 'The Marseillaise' contains the lines: 'Let an impure blood / soak our fields' furrows!'*

6 *Guangzhou (Canton), China.*

7 *Ozone (hole-y).*

8 The Big Lebowski.

9 *Melbourne, Australia.*

10 *Hamburg, Germany.*

CHAPTER 22: 20 AMAZING WOMEN

1 *Maya Angelou.*

2 *Jocelyn Bell Burnell.*

3 *Sirimavo Bandaranaike.*

4 *Karren Brady.*

5 *Elizabeth Fry.*

6 *Malala Yousafzai.*

7 *Dame Tanni (tiny) Grey-Thompson.*

8 *Anne Frank. Anne's father published her diary,* The Secret Annex *in 1947.*

9 *Dame Judi Dench (look up her video rapping with MC Lethal Bizzle, where she wears the rapper's 'Stay Dench' branded baseball cap. Dench* *is slang for 'nice' or 'brilliant', for example in such phrases as: 'Mr Seagull is a dench Maths teacher'.*

10 *Frida Kahlo. Kahlo and Rivera were known as the 'The Elephant and the Dove' due to their difference in size. She is said to have had an affair with Leon Trotsky, who was second only to Lenin in the early stages of Soviet communist rule.*

11 *Sheryl Sandberg.*

12 *Audrey Hepburn. Despite making her role as Holly Golightly in* Breakfast at Tiffany's *absolutely iconic, she was supposedly the author Truman Capote's second choice for the part, behind Marilyn Monroe. And both actresses had dated John F. Kennedy!*

13 *Cathy Freeman.*

14 *Murasaki Shikibu.*

15 *Ada Lovelace. You'll find her buried next to her father, the poet Lord Byron.*

16 *Tracey Emin.*

17 *Nadiya Hussain, who became a national treasure after winning the 2015 series of* The Great British Bake Off. *Sadly she didn't choose 'Everybody (Backstreet's Back)' on* Desert Island Discs – *nobody's perfect.*

18 *Mary Seacole.*

19 *Coco Chanel. She could count – '5' was her first choice, as she was once told by a fortune teller that this was her lucky number.*

20 *Eleanor Roosevelt. Her husband Franklin Delano served as US President.*

CHAPTER 23: 15 OXFORD COLLEGES

1 *St Edmund (the Martyr).*

2 *John de Balliol (or John, King of Scotland), also known as 'Toom Tabard'.*

3 *Merton (Careful! NOT 'Mertonne', as one tonne is 1,000 kilograms).*

4 *Orioles.*

5 *Exeter.*

6 *Hertford.*

7 *The Queen's Gambit.*

8 *All Souls (of the faithful departed). The previous day is All Saints' Day.*

9 *A brass nose. Images of Tycho show him with an enormous moustache covering most of his lower face – even if he'd had a nose, he might not have been able to smell much.*

10 *Corpus Christi, Texas.*

11 *Christchurch, New Zealand.*

12 *The Jesus Lizard (or Jesus Christ Lizard). Again!*

13 *To wad ham.*

14 *Pembroke.*

15 *Worcester.*

CHAPTER 24: 20 6.48AM PUZZLE FOR *TODAY* (AND TOMORROW)

1 *The answer for 6 is Australia. The number represents the number of stars on each national flag (or any other national flag you find can six stars on).*

2 *Birmingham. These are the second largest cities in each country by population.*

3 *511. It is a knockout tournament, and logically only the winner will remain undefeated. Every* *other competitor will lose one, and only one match. So if there are 4 entrants, there will have to be 3 matches, and 3 people have to lose. With 8 entrants, there will be 7 matches and 7 people have to lose. With 128 entrants, there have to be 127 losers, and hence 127 matches. And for 512 participants (as it fits within the model of 2 to the power of* n, *i.e. 2 to the power of 9), you will have 511 losers, so 511 matches.*

4 *Burkina Faso, St Kitts and Nevis, Ethiopia...*
The number represents the number of syllables per word for country names, so there may be other options with five syllables, if you care to find them.

5 *4. It is the number of characters in the opening sentence of Jane Austen's* Pride and Prejudice. *'It is a truth universally acknowledged, that a single man in possession of a good fortune, must be in want of a wife.' The final word 'wife' has 4 characters.*

6 *London. The number represents the number of that summer Games as an Olympiad (e.g. the 1912 Summer Olympics in Stockholm are known as the Games of the V Olympiad). (Note that some numbered Olympiads were cancelled due to war; such as 6, in 1916; and 12 and 13 in 1940 and 1944 respectively.)*

7 *The colours of the Tube lines in this journey are red, orange, yellow, green, blue. If we take the first letters of these colours, this follows the start of the mnemonic 'Richard of York gave battle in vain' to help remember colours of the rainbow. 'Richard of York gave battle in vain' is said to refer to the defeat and death of Richard, Duke of York at* *the Battle of Wakefield in 1460 during the Wars of the Roses. As there are no Tube lines with the colours indigo or violet, this mnemonic would be incomplete and hence a History (or Science) teacher would be feeling frustrated in not being able to complete a theoretical tube journey with these mnemonic colours!*

8 *Each time refers to the official hosting of a FIFA World Cup. It 'happens' when the host nation wins the World Cup. 1 = Uruguay in 1930, 2 = Italy in 1934, 8 = England in 1966, 10 = West Germany in 1974, 11 = Argentina in 1978, 16 = France in 1998. Russia are currently around 40/1 in the bookies for winning their host World Cup in the 21st edition of the 2018 tournament.*

9 *These are US Presidents who were popularly known by their middle or nicknames. Hiram Ulysses Grant went by Ulysses (1869-77), Stephen Grover Cleveland went by Grover (1885-89, 1893-97), Thomas Woodrow Wilson went by Woodrow (1913-21), John Calvin Coolidge Jr went by Calvin (1923-29), James Earl Carter Jr went by Jimmy (1977-81) and William Jefferson Clinton went by Bill (1993-2001).*

10 *24. These are the prime numbers but with one added to them. So 2,3,5,7,11,13,17,19. The next prime number is 23. So the sequence continues with 24.*

11 *The numbers represent the number of colours on a national flag. For a national flag with one colour, the Libyan flag was just a green field until 2011. The country has since re-adopted its flag from 1951 with four colours.*

12 *John is 21. The numbers represent how many points the surnames (such as Humphrys) of the* Today Programme *presenters would gain in a game of Scrabble. Although this would only include the raw points total per letter and exclude any bonus points, such as for using up all your tiles.*

13 *760 is the address of the United Nations Plaza. The other addresses are selected homes of world leaders (5 Adelaide Avenue for the Australian PM, 7 Lok Kalyan Marg is for the Indian PM, 10 Downing Street for the UK PM, 24 Sussex Drive for the Canadian PM, 55 Rue du Faubourg is the Élysée Palace for the French President, 1600 Pennsylvania Ave is the White House for the US President).*

14 *These are countries where the official government currency is the US dollar.*

15 *Rooster. If you line up the animals with years in the Chinese calendar, this particular order will give you the years 1979, 1983, 1987, 1992, 1997, 2001, 2005, 2010, 2015. These are years of UK general elections since 1979, and the next one in sequence is 2017, the Year of the Rooster.*

16 *E. These are the first initials of the names of royals in the line of succession to the monarchy after Queen Elizabeth. Charles, William, George, Charlotte, Harry, Andrew, Beatrice, Eugenie. Next up is Prince Edward, Earl of Wessex.*

17 *These are the traditional wedding anniversary gifts by years since marriage in Britain and the USA. The respective years for Brits and Americans are: 1 year (cotton and paper), 6 years (sugar, iron), 8 years (salt, bronze) and 9 years (copper, pottery).*

18 *1681256. You combine the numerical powers of 2, 3 and 4. So for the first number it is 2 to the power of 1, 3 to the power of 1, 4 to the power of 1 – i.e. 2,3,4 becomes 234. The second number is 2 to the power of 2, 3 to the power of 2 and 4 to the power of 2 i.e. 4, 9, 16 becomes 4916. And so on. So the fourth number is 2 to the power of 4, 3 to the power of 4 and 4 to the power of 4 i.e. 16, 81, 256.*

19 *O. These are the first letter of the numbers in the Fibonacci sequence: 1, 1, 2, 3, 5, 8, 13, 21, 34, 55, 89, 144 ... (The next number is found by adding up the two numbers before it). One, one, two, three, five, eight, thirteen, twenty-one, thirty-four, fifty-five, eighty-nine, one hundred and forty-four.*

20 *These are countries that have periodic table elements named after them. Americium, Copper ('copper' in Latin is 'cuprum'; which was the possible origin of Cyprium, the Roman name for the island of Cyprus), Francium and Gallium and Polonium. Nihonium was named after the common Japanese name for Japan. Dmitri Mendeleev formulated the Periodic Law and created a preliminary version of the periodic table of elements.*

DIFFERENT FORMS OF QUIZ

CHAPTER 25: PUB QUIZ

1 *Burke (Kathy, William, Edmund).*

2 *RSS Sir David Attenborough.*

3 *Cassini (named after Giovanni Domenico Cassini). N.B.: the mission was called the 'Cassini-Huygens Mission', however the Huygens module* *detached and landed on Saturn's largest moon Titan in 2005.*

4 *Iain Sterling.*

5 *King's College.*

6 *Rabbit.*

7 *Damien Hirst.*

8 *Anya Shrubsole.*

9 Game of Thrones.

10 Dead Poets Society.

11 *Strawberries.*

12 Star Trek.

13 *Hero The Hedgehog.*

14 Oliver!

15 *Kent.*

16 *Go (AlphaGo is the programme).*

17 *Matt Cardle.*

18 *Mary Wollstonecraft (mother of Mary Shelley).*

19 Icarus. *Icarus, son of the inventor Daedalus, escaped imprisonment on wings made by his father out of wax. However, in the ecstasy of flight, Icarus flew too close to the sun and his wings melted, causing him to fall into the sea and drown. Success breeding failure, literally.*

20 *Stormzy.*

21 *Virginia Wade.*

22 *The National Trust.*

23 *The O2 Arena, London.*

24 *The FA Cup (formally known as The Football Association Challenge Cup).*

25 *F. Murray Abraham.*

26 *Plato.*

27 *Ivory Coast.*

28 *Plasma (term first introduced by chemist Irving Langmuir in the 1920s).*

29 *Louis Theroux.*

30 *India.*

31 *Bob Marley.*

32 The Guardian *(founded as* 'The Manchester Guardian'*).*

33 Denial.

34 *Hygge (pronounced 'hi-guh').*

35 *Hogwarts. It translates as 'Never Tickle A Sleeping Dragon'.*

36 *Michael Faraday.*

37 *William Blake (title inspired by the line 'Bring me my chariot of fire', adapted into the hymn 'Jerusalem').*

38 *Stephen Fry.*

39 *116 years, from Philip VI's attempt to conquer Guyenne in 1337 to the Battle of Castillon in 1453. Answers from 111 years to 121 years are acceptable.*

40 *The blue whale.*

41 *Egypt.*

42 *Perseus (who cut off Medusa's head; the star is known today as Algol).*

43 *North Korea (it borders South Korea, Russia and China).*

44 *Most recently: Winston Churchill. Born earliest: William Shakespeare. The two greatest Englishmen? Discuss.*

45 *1967 – the centenary of the Canadian Confederation.*

46 The Seagull *(Russian title translates as 'The Gull') and* Swansong *(taken from a short story* *of Chekhov called 'Calchas', after the Ancient Greek seer).*

47 *Lewis Carroll (or Charles Lutwidge Dodgson).*

48 *The fourth wall.*

CHAPTER 26: 10 NEWSPAPER QUIZ

1 *Bantu.*

2 Spirited Away.

3 *John Dowland.*

4 *The weak nuclear force.*

5 *Prince Hamlet and Dr. Faustus, or Faust.*

6 *The South Island of New Zealand (or Te Waipounamu).*

7 *Richard Cromwell.*

8 *Economics.*

9 *Knowledge.*

10 *McGill University.*

CHAPTER 27: 50 PRIMARY SCHOOL–LEVEL QUESTIONS

HISTORY

1 *Skara Brae.*

2 *Claudius.*

3 *Edward the Confessor.*

4 *Rosetta Stone.*

5 *Elizabeth I.*

6 *Tim Berners-Lee.*

7 *The Great Fire of London.*

8 *Mayans.*

GEOGRAPHY

1 *Ben Nevis.*

2 *The Prime Meridian line.*

3 *Ordnance Survey ('ordnance' means mounted guns or artillery; locations of artillery in Scotland were mapped by the British military after the Jacobite rebellion in 1745, and called 'ordnance maps').*
4 *Tectonic plates.*
5 *Indonesia.*
6 *Tropic of Capricorn (or Southern Tropic).*

♑

MATHS
1 *180-40 =140. 140 divided by 2 = 70 degrees for missing angles.*
2 *René Descartes.*
3 *160 (320 preferred Beyoncé).*
4 *24 (2 x 3 x 4). Or one for every hour of the day, and no friends.*
5 *West.*
6 *1.21m.*

ENGLISH
1 *Pangram.*
2 Beowulf.
3 *Palindrome.*
4 *They use their initials rather than their full names (AA Milne, CS Lewis, JK Rowling and JRR Tolkien).*
5 *Alliteration.*
6 *They are known as homophones. As opposed to 'homonyms' which are words pronounced and spelled the same way, but have different meaning; for example 'book' (a pageturner) and 'book' (to schedule an event or reservation).*

SCIENCE

1. *Dwarf planet (just a little bit bigger than Snow White's dwarves).*
2. *Stigma.*
3. *Reptiles.*
4. *Liver.*
5. *Centripetal force.*
6. *Sedimentary.*
7. *Series.*
8. *Vaporisation.*
9. *Chloroplasts.*

MUSIC

1. *Mars. The BBC's third set of* Ten Pieces *includes an a capella piece by Kerry Andrew titled 'No Place Like'. Watch this performance on http://www.bbc.co.uk/programmes/p05dtp73. (Kerry Andrew also writes one of the best and wittiest* University Challenge *weekly blog reviews! Find on universitychallenged.tumblr.com.)*
2. *Beatboxing.*
3. *Brass.*

ART, DESIGN & TECHNOLOGY

1. *Collage.*
2. Bayeux Tapestry.
3. *Lever or fulcrum.*

RELIGION

1. *Hinduism.*
2. *Mount Sinai.*
3. *The Buddha.*

MODERN FOREIGN LANGUAGES

1 *The (English) Channel.*
2 *Spain (red, yellow, red in Spanish and Catalan).*
3 *Panda.*

COMPUTING

1 *Digital native.*
2 *Debug. In 1947, an actual moth inside a computer was found to have stopped it from working!*
3 *Pixel.*

CHRISTMAS

CHAPTER 28: 20 ALL I WANT FOR CHRISTMAS IS... CHRISTMAS-THEMED QUIZ QUESTIONS

1 *Marley (Jacob Marley, Bob Marley and* Marley & Me*).*
2 *Oslo.*
3 *These were all Christmas number one singles in the United Kingdom – Christmas music can be more than carols and Cliff Richard.*
4 *These are the names of the Three Wise Men (Blunt's song is 'Wisemen').*
5 *They all sang the first line.*
6 *1932.*
7 *5 gold rings (12 x 4 = 48. 48 + 2 = 50. 50 divided by 10 = 5).*
8 *D. There are three: Dasher, Dancer, Donner. Next would be C as there are two – Comet and Cupid. The others are Prancer, Vixen and Blitzen. (Rudolph is sometimes famously known as the ninth reindeer, as he was created by American Robert May in 1939.)*

9 *KFC (the phrase means 'Kentucky for Christmas!').*

10 *Cake (cold, Anna, Kristoff, Elsa).*

11 *HOH OHO.*

12 *Dublin, Ireland.*

13 *Washington's crossing of the Delaware (it was followed by the Battle of Trenton).*

14 *The Julian calendar (or Old Style calendar).*

15 *The Commonwealth of Australia.*

16 *The (First) Council of Nicaea ('the Nicene Creed' is close enough).*

17 *The Battle of Naseby.*

18 *Prague, Czech Republic.*

19 *Hair combs.*

20 *Twenty-five.*

THE FINAL CHALLENGE

CHAPTER 29: FINAL 40 BUZZER-STYLE TRIVIA TOSSUPS (10 SETS OF 4 QUESTIONS)

TOSSUP 1: *Nicolaus Copernicus.*

1 *Shinzō Abe.*

2 *Hirobumi Itō.*

3 *Yuriko Koike.*

TOSSUP 2: *Endangered species.*

1 *Kabul (Afghanistan) and cabal (the Cabal ministry included Baron Clifford, the Earl of Arlington, the Duke of Buckingham, Baron Ashley and the Duke of Lauderdale).*

2 *Bern (or Berne, Switzerland) and burn.*

3 *Seoul (Korea) and sole.*

TOSSUP 3: *Goya (or Francisco José de Goya y Lucientes).*

1 *Gresham's Law.*

2 *(Ricardo's) Theory of Comparative Advantage.*

3 *The quantity theory of money.*

Tossup 4: *Abraham Lincoln.*

1 The Mikado *(or* The Town of Titipu*).*

2 Iolanthe *(or* The Peer and the Peri*).*

3 The Pirates of Penzance *(or* The Slave of Duty*).*

TOSSUP 5: *Mary Magdalene (or Mary of Magdala).*

1 *Atahualpa.*

2 *Tecumseh.*

3 *Montezuma (or Moctezuma II).*

TOSSUP 6: *The Trinity test of the atomic bomb.*

1 *The Burghers of Calais.*

2 *The Judgement of Paris.*

3 *Cicero denouncing Catiline (or the Catiline Orations).*

TOSSUP 7: *Sir Robert Menzies (he was of Scottish heritage).*

1 *Bowerbirds.*

2 *Tuataras.*

3 *The Tasmanian devil.*

TOSSUP 8: *The University.*

1 *Veni, vidi, vici (which translates to 'I came, I saw, I conquered.') Jan III Sobieski's message attributed the victory to God ('Deus vicit', or 'God conquered').*

2 *'I fear the Greeks, though gift on gift they* bear' *(from Theodore C. Williams's translation). 'Beware of Greeks bearing gifts' is more frequently used in English.*

3 *'This' or 'these'. The words in the motto are 'this (man)', 'this (woman)', 'this (thing)', 'these (men)', 'these (women)' and 'these (things)'.*

TOSSUP 9: *Hans Christian Andersen.*

1 *Joseph Lister (or Lord Lister). He served as President of the Royal Society from 1895 to 1900.*

2 *Huxley. Andrew Huxley, who experimented with squid nerve cells, was President from 1980 to 1985. Thomas Henry Huxley, 'Darwin's bulldog', was President from 1883 to 1885.*

3 *Sir Isaac Newton.*

TOSSUP 10: *Fibonacci (or Leonardo of Pisa; or Leonardo Pisano. Fibonacci was likely used as a short form of Filius Bonacci, or 'son of a Bonaccio', after his father).*

1 *Rill and grill (Supposedly, when St Lawrence was being roasted to death, he told his tormentors to turn him over because he was done on that side. He is now the patron saint of comedians).*

2 *Turin and Turing.*

3 *Baring and Barging.*

CONCLUSION

'Now, what I want is, facts.
Teach these boys and girls nothing but facts.
Facts alone are wanted in life.'
So your final question in this book is: Who do these words belong to? (HINT: They are spoken by the headmaster in the Charles Dickens novel *Hard Times*.)
The answer is... (see final page...)

Well, we don't think facts are the *only* thing that are wanted in life, but they can be fun. Whether you're a young reader, new to quizzing or a pub quiz wizard, we hope that people of all skills and interests can gain something from this book – both knowledge and enjoyment.
Now, if you're flicking through this book and have skipped to the conclusion: stop right here! Go back into the book and crack on with the questions!
If you've actually gone through the quiz book and managed to survive till the very end: well done! We hope that you enjoyed this Monkman & Seagull quizzing adventure, and if you had half the fun we had answering the questions as we have had in writing them, you'll have had a blast!

ACKNOWLEDGEMENTS

Eric Monkman would like to acknowledge the support he received while writing this book from his family, including Debby Badowski, Katie Monkman and Jean Badowski. He would like to thank Fraser Simpson for helpful advice. He is also grateful to his agents, Sally Harding and Dean Cooke.

Both of us would like to thank our agent on this book, Robert Gwyn Palmer, for his guidance, encouragement and initiative. And of course everyone at Eyewear. Todd Swift for having the vision of making a quiz book and his wonderful team, Rosanna Hildyard, Alexandra Payne and Edwin Smet. Thanks also to Helen McCusker from Booked PR for helping us to spread the news about our book. Eyewear wants to thank Suetonius the cat-editor for his attention to detail.

...*Mr Gradgrind*, of course.